Praise for *Job Search Bloopers*

"This book is fascinating! Reading people's stories makes you want to laugh or cry, but Laura and Susan do a masterful job pulling learning moments together to help us understand what we can avoid to have a successful job search. This will be a must-have on any career bookshelf!"

> —Jason Alba, CEO of JibberJobber.com and author of *I'm on LinkedIn…Now What?*

"What a brilliant concept—learning from mistakes that others have made rather than committing your own career 'bloopers.' In an entertaining format that is also highly insightful and educational, Laura and Susan have zeroed in on the common mistakes that derail so many career moves. Whatever your age, level, or profession, you will gain helpful information that will keep your job search—and your career—moving forward."

> —Louise Kursmark, author of *30-Minute Resume Makeover* and 20 additional books on career management

"With *Job Search Bloopers*, Susan Guarneri and Laura DeCarlo have created the perfect resource for the frustrated job-seeker who wonders 'Why can't I get a job?', 'What am I doing wrong?', or 'Why am I so miserable in my career?' The book's structure, which offers job-seeker stories, pinpoints exactly how the job-seeker has stumbled, and clearly outlines a better strategy, could not be more user-friendly. Guarneri and DeCarlo then motivate the reader by spelling out steps for a more effective job search. It's one thing to read the same old advice from career experts; it's quite another to learn from the impact of this book's stories."

> —Katharine Hansen, PhD, Associate Publisher and Creative Director of Quintessential Careers, and author of *Top Notch Executive Resumes*

"This practical book by Susan Guarneri and Laura DeCarlo lives up to its recommendations for readers in providing value (benefits that readers need) and great tips on personal branding. As a useful job search book, this one is at the front of the pack."

—David F. Noble, PhD, best-selling author of *Gallery of Best Resumes*

"Laura DeCarlo and Susan Guarneri offer a practical, down-to-earth guide to job search success. By citing real-life examples of how job seekers have unwittingly torpedoed their chances, *Job Search Bloopers* allows readers the opportunity to learn from someone else's mistakes and avoid making their own. A must-read for anyone engaged in an active job search."

—Arnold Boldt, CPRW, JCTC, author of *No-Nonsense Job Interviews* and *Resumes for the Rest of Us*

"Susan Guarneri and Laura DeCarlo know how to cut through the clutter and share the real secrets of successfully managing your career or job search. Packed with real-life 'blooper' stories that illustrate the most common pitfalls, this book is your inside track to making all the right moves. The authors dissect and demystify prevalent job search and career concerns with in-depth analysis and cutting-edge recommendations—including demonstrating the role personal branding plays in career success. If you're stuck in your job search or puzzled about your next career move, this book will provide the boost you need!"

—William Arruda, the Personal Branding Guru and author of the best-selling *Career Distinction: Stand Out by Building Your Brand*

JOB SEARCH
BLOOPERS

Every Mistake You Can
Make on the Road to
Career Suicide...
and How to Avoid Them

Laura DeCarlo
and
Susan Guarneri

CAREER
PRESS
Franklin Lakes, NJ

Copyright © 2008 by Laura DeCarlo and Susan Guarneri

Cartoons used with permission of artist Steven Lait.

JOB SEARCH BLOOPERS
EDITED BY JODI BRANDON
TYPESET BY EILEEN DOW MUNSON
Cover design by Lu Rossman / Digi Dog Design NY
Printed in the U.S.A. by Book-mart Press

To order this title, please call toll-free 1-800-CAREER-1 (NJ and Canada: 201-848-0310) to order using VISA or MasterCard, or for further information on books from Career Press.

The Career Press, Inc., 3 Tice Road, PO Box 687,
Franklin Lakes, NJ 07417
www.careerpress.com

Library of Congress Cataloging-in-Publication Data
DeCarlo, Laura.
   Job search bloopers : every mistake you can make on the
road to career suicide—and how to avoid them / by Laura
DeCarlo and Susan Guarneri.
      p.cm.
   Includes index.
   ISBN 978-1-60163-016-2
      1. Job hunting. I. Guarneri, Susan. II. Title.

HF5382.7.D425 2008
650.14--dc22

2008011631

Contents

Authors' Note 7

Introduction 9

Chapter 1: Job Application Avalanche 13

Chapter 2: Résumé Writing Roadblocks 25

Chapter 3: Cover Letter Casualties 73

Chapter 4: Follow-Up Letter Follies 89

Chapter 5: Job Search Jinxes 101

Chapter 6: Networking Nightmares 143

Chapter 7: Common Job Curses 159

Chapter 8: Interviewing Inadequacies 179

Chapter 9: Slippery Salary Slopes 215

Chapter 10: Job Reference Rejects 225

Appendix A: List of Contributors 233

Appendix B: Career Directors International 241

Appendix C: Cited Online Resources 243

Appendix D: References 249

Index 251

About the Authors 255

Authors' Note

Who Contributed to the Book?

Many of the "stories" in this book come from the members of Career Directors International, a professional association for career-industry professionals. A listing of these contributors from across the United States, Australia, and Canada can be found in Appendix A. We want to acknowledge their generosity in submitting their stories and accompanying recommended strategies.

Introduction

Job Search Bloopers is a one-of-a-kind book that seeks to educate, entertain, and inform the job seeker on a broad range of highly common job search mistakes. But, more importantly, for every story that makes you moan, groan, or secretly acknowledge you have been there yourself, there is a critical lesson to be learned on what not to do, and—better yet—*how to do it right the first time.*

Put the stories end-to-end and you have powerful strategies across the spectrum of document development (job applications, résumé writing, cover letter writing, follow-up letter writing, and references), interviewing and salary negotiation, career management/job selection, and job search and networking. Whether you choose to slide down slippery salary slopes or overcome cover letter casualties, you will find the tools in this entertaining book to help you.

Why This Book—And Why Now?

With the world of work becoming increasingly complex due to change of every sort, the one constant we can depend on is making mistakes or "bloopers." Because no one is perfect (well, most of us anyway), every goal we set is fraught with the danger of failure. These mistakes, both big and small, are painfully evident in the realm of the job search.

If it were easy to land a "dream job" or "dream promotion," everyone would presumably be a "quality match" with their job. Job dissatisfaction would be low, productivity would be high, and turnover and talent acquisition would not be the ever-prevalent issues they are for employers. We know from the high numbers of employees who are actively seeking other employment, as much as 70 percent according to recent surveys, that such is not the case.

The main premise of this book is that learning from mistakes is critical to improving your chances for job search success. Why re-invent the wheel? By reading the "blooper" stories in this book, along with the alternative recommendations and resources, you can leap across the chasm of these common job-seeker mistakes and avoid them altogether. It is possible to move smoothly from one great job to another as your needs and desires warrant. Hopefully, the insights and strategies you gain from these stories will put you on the "dream career" pathway a lot sooner!

Can You Benefit From This Book?

Anyone who is interested in exploring and improving their career and employment possibilities, and conducting a successful job search in less time, would benefit from reading this book. We believe this could be vast segments of the population, including all generations (Baby Boomer, Gen X, Gen Y, and Millennial).

Whether you are an entry-level applicant, a teenager, a new college graduate, a blue/green/white-collar worker, a mid-to upper-level manager, or an executive, the principles and "best practices" cited in this book will allow you to skip the "learning curve" of experiential job search knowledge in favor of a fast-track to job-search fulfillment. You may be seeking your first job, or perhaps your last before (or during) retirement. Maybe you want a career or job change, full-time or part-time employment, or something meaningful (that also pays well) for retirement. If so, make this book your roadmap; you are the audience this book was meant to serve.

How Is This Book Organized?

The book contains 72 "blooper" stories organized into 10 chapters, each covering a different aspect of the job-search and career-promotion process (see the Contents).

Though any one of the "bloopers" showcased in the 72 stories can derail a job search, some areas in particular seem laden with plentiful pitfalls. That's why you will notice that three chapters—résumés (Chapter 2), job search (Chapter 5), and interviewing (Chapter 8)—are longer than others.

The stories within each chapter have three parts: Job Seeker's Story, Job Seeker's Stumble, and Job Seeker's New Strategy. The first part (Job Seeker's Story) encapsulates the actual "blooper" and outcome, the second (Job Seeker's Stumble) isolates what went wrong, and the final part (Job Seeker's New Strategy) highlights recommended alternative actions. Resources and links are provided, as well as "how-to" information on preventing the "blooper" from happening to you!

What Can You Do to Get the Most Out of This Book?

You may first choose to read the book from cover to cover and note entries of relevancy and interest to your situation. Or selecting topics that you are currently struggling with may seem the better approach for you.

In either case, you will find that "refreshing" your knowledge regarding a topic (for example, interviewing and salary negotiations) will be helpful whether you are a first-time job seeker or a veteran of many job-search campaigns. Learn from the mistakes of others in the 72 stories presented, all based on real incidents that have been made anonymous for confidentiality reasons.

To reinforce what you have learned, read the book first, and then discuss it with another job seeker. You may want to enlarge that social network into a job search group. Besides discussing the book, share stories and construct customized strategies and action plans for each member of the group. Always re-evaluate your strategies and plans after using them to fine-tune the job-search process. Finally—celebrate successes!

CHAPTER *1*

Job Application Avalanche

^

First Impressions Count—In Person and on Paper
Job Seeker's Story

Tim had been asked to fill out an application prior to being scheduled for an interview, so he decided to drop by and pick it up on his way to play tennis with his new girlfriend, Suzie. He assumed he would slip in relatively unnoticed, so it would not matter that he was wearing scuffed and worn tennis shoes and cutoff shorts.

When they arrived, Suzie went in with Tim because she was excited to see where he would be working. When they arrived, the secretary looked them both over, noting that they were holding hands, and asked, *"Can I help you?"*

Tim replied, *"Yes. I need to pick up a job application."*

"Certainly," said the secretary, *"Your name?"*

Surprised, Tim said, *"My name is Tim Jones."*

"Who are you interviewing with?" she then asked.

"Umm, I didn't bring that information with me," said Tim, frowning now.

"Just a minute. I'll call back to Human Resources and find out," she said, and picked up the phone.

Finally, the secretary made a few notes and handed him a clipboard and application, telling Tim to fill it out and return it to her before leaving.

Feeling panicked, Tim asked if he could take it home and return it to her the following day. She looked at him for the longest time (at least a minute, Tim thought) before she responded, *"I am sorry, but we do not allow applications to leave the building. It's policy."*

Tim sat down to fill out the application and realized he did not have a pen, he had not brought his résumé, and he did not remember the dates he worked in his prior positions, phone numbers for supervisors, or how many credits he had earned toward his master's degree. He was rattled and unprepared, but he did his best to fill out the application.

Tim had expected to be able to look up dates and tailor descriptions at home. His mind was a blank and he ended up leaving sections (supervisor phone numbers, for example) blank, and feeling flustered, so he made errors and wrote short, ineffective descriptions. He did his best, but his application ended up messy and rather incomplete.

Leaving, Tim felt disappointed and wished he had done things differently. He was not surprised when he did no get a call back to return for an interview.

Job Seeker's Stumble

Poor Tim had the best intentions, but he made several mistakes that could have been easily remedied. He:

▷ Arrived unprepared to fill out the application on the spot with a pen and detailed chronology of his work history and former employer information.

▷ Made the mistake of not recognizing that his attire and choice to bring a friend along would not demonstrate professionalism or leave a positive impression.

▷   Prepared an application that was incomplete, messy, and lacking detail.

Job Seeker's ≥New Strategy≤

Every impression you make—on the phone, walking in to request or fill out an application, or interviewing for a job—counts when you are a candidate for employment. The best advice is to be prepared when entering a place of employment, as if you are going to be interviewed. Specifically:

▷   **Dress for Success:** Wear the level of attire you would select if you were being interviewed.

▷   **Bring Sufficient Documentation:** The easiest way to handle the job application is to bring all the information typically required in a job application. This includes:

> Detailed job descriptions written to target the job currently being sought.

> Company names, addresses, phone numbers, and supervisor names.

> Dates of employment, including month and year.

> Education and training history, including relevant courses, number of credits, dates of attendance, school names, and degrees/certifications.

> A list of all special skills relevant to the position.

▷   **Be Prepared:** Along with your documentation, be sure to bring erasable pens, paper correction fluid, copies of your résumé, and copies of your references. You should also bring an application addendum if you have legal issues such as a felony, which will be addressed on the application.

▷   **Respect the Gatekeepers:** Do not forget that those you interact with in the office can be the gatekeepers who can make or break your success with the employer. Additionally, always go alone when visiting a prospective employer's place of business.

▷ **Target the Job:** Make sure that you do not rely on one-size-fits-all application responses when filling out key skills and employment experience sections. Take the approach of target marketing for the job you want, and emphasize your strengths and experience instead of just listing everything.

▷ **Keep it Neat:** Your best choice is to read the application fully before you begin to fill it out to ensure you place information in the correct spaces and avoid ending up with a messy document.

It is easy to make a positive first impression if you plan and prepare as if you are going to the interview when requesting or filling out an application!

A Résumé Does Not Replace an Application

Job Seeker's Story

Beverley felt confident as she arrived at her interview for an operations management position. She had dressed professionally, researched the company, prepared questions to ask, and had printed extra copies of her résumé on fine linen paper, which she had placed in her attaché case.

The office was busy and she had to wait several minutes for the receptionist to get to her. She was handed a job application to fill out while she waited to meet with her interviewer, Mr. Simpson. Beverley accepted the application and returned to her seat.

Ten minutes later Beverley was directed to the office of Mr. Simmons, who accepted the job application. After glancing at it for a few seconds, he said, *"Why didn't you fill this out?"*

Beverley said, *"Well, I am here for a management position, so I just assumed your receptionist made a mistake."*

Mr. Simmons replied, *"We require all applicants to fill out the application. We'll have to reschedule your appointment since I don't have the time to wait for you to do this now."*

Surprised, Beverley replied, *"I don't see why that is neces-sary; you already have my résumé. Can't we just go from that and speak now?"*

Standing up, Mr. Simmons opened the door and said, *"Ms. Jones, your unwillingness to follow a simple request and to ques-tion it when given a second chance leads me to believe you will not be a good fit for this organization. Thank you for your time."*

Beverley continued to sit as a smile slowly spread across your face. She leaned forward and said, *"I get it: You're kidding, right?"*

Mr. Simmons looked at her with his lips pursed tightly. He said, *"This isn't a TV show. I'm not joking, and I'm not going to interview you. This meeting is over."* He crossed his arms and stood in the doorway until Beverley picked up her attaché case and walked quickly out of the office.

The next day Beverley tried to reach Mr. Simmons to apolo-gize and even sent a follow-up letter reiterating the request for a second chance. Unfortunately for her, her calls and letter received no response.

Job Seeker's Stumble

Beverley's errors should be clear: She did not follow direc-tions, was inflexible, and felt her position level meant she was above having to fill out a job application.

Job Seeker's ≥New Strategy≤

This might seem to be a simple blooper, but, surpris-ingly, it has been one of the top reasons that middle man-agers and higher have been excluded from consideration by companies. An unwillingness to follow directions and an at-titude of being above what is asked of you never makes a posi-tive impression on a prospective employer. An interviewer/employer will think this entitlement attitude is what they can expect from you on the job!

Additionally, there are well-founded reasons to require an applicant to fill out and sign a job application. For instance, when you fill out and sign a job application, you provide an employer with the legal ability to be able to verify the information you have provided. Also, if an employer has a practice of collecting applications from candidates, then it is necessary that they do this consistently with each and every applicant, regardless of position level. Otherwise, an audit could uncover this as an issue in providing equal employment opportunities.

Just follow this simple advice: When you are being evaluated as an applicant for an employment position, show a go-to, team-player attitude by following instructions.

Get It There—And Then Follow Up

Job Seeker's Story

With 11 years of experience in the telecommunications industry as an information technology (IT) specialist, Jerry desperately wanted to land a job with a local government agency. So he invested in a résumé writing professional to assist him in formulating his application materials (résumé and cover letter).

Two days before the deadline, the entire application was ready, and met all the rules and requirements for submission. The application process offered the choice of delivery via a hard copy or electronically via e-mail to the organization's generic e-mail address. Jerry elected to use technology as his preferred method of delivery, as this application was for an IT specialist position.

Although coached to follow up immediately, Jerry waited for three weeks. He discovered that his application, sent well before the closing date, had not been received. Interviews were underway, and a decision was imminent. The Human Resources manager apologized and then freely admitted to a glitch in the organization's e-mail system for processing online applications, which had now been rectified. That was the good news; the bad news was that Jerry was not even considered for his "ideal" position, although he met all the job-posting requirements.

Job Seeker's Stumble

This example clearly demonstrates the devastating effect of neglecting the simple, yet essential, step of confirming receipt of your application and following up in a timely way on its progress throughout the decision-making cycle.

Job Seeker's ≷New Strategy≷

Confirmation of receipt and follow-up on your application are vital. Follow these guidelines when submitting applications for advertised vacancies:

▷ **Preferred Method:** Check with the company or organization on the preferred method and format for your application. Several possibilities include:

> Microsoft Word document attached to a job-application e-mail.

> Plain-text (ASCII) content submitted into form fields on the job-opening's Web page.

> Hard copy application mailed to the company's office.

> Plain-text (ASCII) document copied in the body of a job-posting response e-mail.

> Hand-delivering the hard-copy application materials.

Can you submit your application in more than one way to ensure receipt?

▷ **Compatibility:** If a MS Word document is required, find out what version the organization uses. You will be wasting effort and valuable time if you are using MS Word 2007 and the company is still using MS Word 2000 or 2003. Not everyone has kept up-to-date with the most recent release of word-processing software programs.

▷ **Timeliness:** If sending your application by mail, do so well in advance of the closing date, and do not guess about the postage required. Registered mail and/or express delivery are great ideas to avoid missing out or having your application lost somewhere in transit; plus, you can get proof of delivery.

　　If sending by e-mail, allow enough advance time to overcome hiccups or glitches in your or the recipient's e-mail program, and to address unforeseen problems such as power failures, storms, and Internet service provider (ISP) interruptions. Be one of the first e-mailed responses to the job posting, rather than the last. In some cases, companies will only look at the first 100 (or less) applications!

▷ **Confirmation:** Find out if your application was received when e-mailing it to a generic e-mail address (such as jobs@companyname.com) or through a company or organization's Website. If it was mailed, follow up with a call saying you are checking on the status of your application.

　　Avoid relying on auto-responder programs to confirm receipt of your application, even if the company or organization states this is how it will make contact with you. Although you may have great confidence in communications and information technology, it never hurts to pick up the phone and ask for confirmation. However, if a job posting or ad specifies "no calls," you will do best to honor that request.

▷ **Attachment Accessibility:** Verify that the receiver was able to open the attachment. If it could not be opened, you now have the opportunity to send your application another way before the application deadline.

▷ **Application Progress:** Once your application is confirmed as received, relax and take a short breather. Now, open your daily planner and schedule a follow-up of your application's progress.

The time frame usually depends on the size of the company or organization, and its recruitment policy and procedures. It is always a good idea to obtain an estimate of how long the application-review process may take when confirming that your e-mail or printed document has been received. For a small company or privately owned business, it may be three to five days; for a medium-sized company, or government or community-based organization, one to two weeks is more typical. For a larger organization, the review and short-listing process can take substantially longer.

Do follow up with the designated contact person for the position, which is usually found on the advertisement, or speak to someone in the Human Resources department. Ask whether applications for the position have been reviewed yet. If not, find out when you can expect to be advised of your application's progress, and then schedule a second follow-up reminder.

If you are unable to find out any definite details, send a follow-up letter to demonstrate your continued interest and strong candidacy. Present additional information not provided in your first application, to further strengthen your case for an interview.

▷ **Thanks:** In all of your follow-up calls, be sure to convey your thanks, even if you are not invited to interview. Then seize the opportunity to elicit specific feedback and information about what you can do to improve your chances next time, as well as demonstrate your ongoing interest in the company or organization.

The major lesson from this story: Never assume that your message will land in the right hands, even when a prospective employer has an auto-responder program or stipulates that you will be contacted by e-mail or letter. To avoid the pain of missing out on your dream job and for peace of mind, there is nothing wrong with picking up the telephone and making personal contact with someone who can check—just to make sure!

Humor Gone Awry

Job Seeker's Story

This was Jeff's first real interview for a full-time job right out of college. He knew the Insurance Policy Services position was an entry-level job, and had prepared for the interview by doing a little Internet research on Global Insurance a few days earlier. It was a solid company and looked to be a great place to begin getting some career experience.

The interview seemed to be going well. Although Jeff faltered on some questions, he felt sure that his self-confidence and smooth communications skills would make him a top candidate for this position. As the half-hour interview wound down, the interviewer seemed to pause as he turned the application over and saw what Jeff had filled in for "Salary Desired."

With a puzzled look, the interviewer asked, *"I see that you have indicated a desired salary of one million dollars. Is that accurate?"*

Looking directly into the interviewer's eyes, Jeff responded confidently, *"Doesn't everyone think he's worth a million dollars?"*

Standing up and offering his hand, the interviewer responded, *"I see…. Interesting. Well, that's all the information that we need at this time. Thank you for coming. We will be in touch if you are selected for a follow-up interview."*

Jeff shook the interviewer's hand and positively beamed. He never imagined how easy interviews could be.

However, the interviewer was of another opinion. After Jeff had gone, the interviewer remarked to one of his colleagues, *"That one was acting like a clown. Imagine, asking for a million-dollar salary for an entry-level job! That's really the frosting on the cake! He displayed very little knowledge about the insurance industry, and even less about what the Insurance Policy Services position entails."*

Job Seeker's Stumble

Jeff's attempt at humor fell flat and resulted in no follow-up by Global Insurance. He had not gauged the industry or the interviewer appropriately. Although humor can be effective in some interview situations, use it carefully, especially when dealing with a critical issue like salary.

Job Seeker's ≥New Strategy≤

There are other ways Jeff could have handled the "Salary Desired" question on the application, any of which would probably been better in this case. For example:

▷ **Leave Open for Discussion:** You can do this by putting "Open," "Negotiable," or "To be discussed in the interview" on the application form. After getting a better sense of the job duties and finding out the salary range offered by the company, Jeff could have positioned himself positively by indicating that his desired salary range and the company's salary range did indeed overlap. Because salary is often used as a screening-out device, indicating a specific salary ahead of time on the application or in a cover letter, without knowing the company's ballpark range, can be thought of as trying to hit the bull's-eye on a target while blindfolded.

▷ **List a Well-Researched Salary Range:** Use Internet resources to research the competitive salary range for the position. Further refine the research by using factors such as the type of industry, years of experience, and the geographical location of the job (for example, East Coast or West Coast). You can Google the term *salary research* or *salary search* to find many Websites that offer this kind of information. For example, Salary.com, WageWeb.com, SalaryWizard.com, Careerexperience.com, SalaryMaster.com, and PayScale.com are commonly used.

Take the extra step of researching salaries for the industry, position, and geographic region prior to your first interview. Armed with that knowledge, you can judge if the employer's initial offer is competitive or not. Do not limit your salary up front without knowing as much as you can about the potential job, including the salary.

Though more in-depth salary negotiations typically take place at the second or subsequent interviews, do not jeopardize your chances of getting to that stage by over-pricing yourself out of a follow-up interview. Even worse, do not undervalue yourself; even if hired, you will soon regret that strategy, and continue to regret it with every paycheck.

CHAPTER 2

Résumé Writing Roadblocks

⌃

Be Selective and Careful With Your Résumé Content

Job Seeker's Story

Merle had worked for 22 years as a Social Worker at various local non-profit and government human-services agencies. In her last job with the county family-services agency, she was promoted to Senior Social Worker with a large caseload. She had been hired throughout her career on the recommendation of friends and professional colleagues who were employees and, thus, had never had to have a résumé—until now. With the advent of automation and economic tough times for social-services agencies, Merle's job was eliminated, and she was in the job market for the first time in a long time. As many job seekers do, Merle realized she needed a résumé as soon as possible. These are some of the items Merle included in her brand-new résumé:

▷ E-mail address: IHearVoices@xxx.com.

▷ Education: bachelor's degree in social work (BSW) dated 23 years ago, with no continuing professional development or certifications listed.

▷ Complete job history covering 10 jobs over 22 years with details of job duties and responsibilities for each.

▷ Footnotes to her job history, citing more information that could be obtained and where, including names of people, addresses, and phone numbers.

▷ Computer skills: Windows 95, MS Office 95.

▷ Community involvement: Pen Pal Program (PPP) with State Division of Corrections facility inmates over 12-year period.

▷ Hobbies: bungee jumping, para-gliding, Internet dating, and exotic dancing.

▷ Awards: Most Bungee Jumps in 2007 (Over-50 Category)—National Bungee Jumpers Association.

▷ Detailed salary history and reasons for leaving each job (in many cases multiple reasons for leaving just one job).

▷ Twelve references (covering her jobs going back 22 years), as well as their home and business contact information (addresses, phone numbers, and e-mail addresses).

Merle's fully loaded résumé printed out at 10 pages. She had worked hard over six weeks to verify and acquire all the information. By including every detail of her career, Merle felt sure someone somewhere would sift through all of the information provided in the résumé and see a "match" with what his or her organization needed.

Merle opted to print 20 copies of her résumé on good paper. *"Surely,"* she thought, *"I won't need more than 20? After all, I got my previous jobs fairly quickly before, and those without even having a résumé!"*

Job Seeker's Stumble

Merle may be doomed to a protracted and perhaps even unsuccessful job search due to the content she chose to include in her résumé. Although much of it is résumé overkill, other aspects are inappropriate and off-base, raising more questions about Merle's suitability to be entrusted with another position of responsibility in social work.

Job Seeker's ≷New Strategy≷

A résumé does need to reflect your career history accurately, but it also must be a selective marketing document. What you choose to eliminate and include can make or break your chances of being considered as a serious applicant by employment reviewers. Let's analyze each of the bulleted points in Merle's story (pages 25–26) to determine a more marketable and reader-friendly document. Each bullet point represents a glaring mistake, any one of which can be fatal for a résumé:

▷ **Questionable E-Mail Address:** Changing her e-mail address from IHearVoices@xxx.com was absolutely critical to Merle's professional credibility. Upon urging from her friends and career coach, Merle decided to use MPearceBSW@xxx.com, which reflected both her name and professional status. Cutesy, objectionable, or hair-raising e-mail addresses may seem funny, but for job search purposes must be avoided. Do not raise red flags before the reviewer has even read your résumé. In fact, your résumé will most likely end up in the reviewer's spam folder due to the questionable nature of the e-mail address.

▷ **Education:** Because a BSW is the minimum requirement for a Social Worker position, it was essential that Merle list it on her résumé. However, including the date the degree was granted reminded the reviewer that Merle's training in the field was old, and who buys old knowledge? Also, Merle did not list her social work certifications, licenses, and professional development, which leaves the reviewer to assume she did not have any certification or up-to-date training. The quick fix for this section was simply to eliminate the date of the "old" degree, list Merle's recent (past five years) professional development seminars and courses by topic, and prominently display her licenses and certifications. These professional-development topic titles, licenses, and certifications are often keywords that employment reviewers deem required for an applicant to make the cut to candidate.

▷ **Job History:** Detailing 22 years of work experience is an information "dump" and résumé overkill. No one would spend the time reading 10 pages of the stuff—probably not even Merle's mother! One of the really difficult challenges in writing your own résumé is having the objectivity and insight to realize what is relevant to the job target you are pursuing, and to eliminate (or greatly minimize) what is not. Covering the most recent 10–15 years on a résumé is sufficient, unless there is compelling evidence to make your case in an earlier time period (perhaps within the past 20 years). Do not date yourself with "ancient history"; employment reviewers need to know how you have handled the multiple challenges of the *modern* work world with all of the inherent technological and social challenges in your recent jobs.

▷ **Footnotes:** This one is easy: Simply do not list them. Again, this level of detail in a résumé is just not needed. If an employment reviewer feels a detailed explanation is needed for anything on the résumé, he will ask!

▷ **Computer/Technology Skills:** It is important to list computer skills if you have them, but you do not want to showcase old computer skills. This is a tip-off to the employment reviewer that Merle has not kept up-to-date with the world of technology, and begs the question about what else she has not kept up-to-date on (such as her education and continuing professional development). The possible fixes here are, in the short run, to eliminate Computer Skills as a category (it is doing more damage right now than helping), and, in the long run, to acquire training on the latest computer software used most often in Merle's occupation, and then list them in this category.

▷ **Community Involvement/Leadership:** This can definitely be an asset on your résumé if chosen wisely. For Merle it leaves the employment reviewer wondering, *"Hmmm.... Why exactly has she been communicating with a prison inmate* *or inmates for the past 12 years? Does this demonstrate lack of judgment in someone who would hold a position of trust and confidentiality?"* Merle has a couple of options:

1. She can eliminate this item from her résumé.

2. She can highlight her leadership in pioneering the county social services department Pen Pal Program that connected families of inmates with their loved ones and that the warden cited as "the linchpin factor in the declining rate of recidivism in the county."

▷ **Hobbies and Awards:** Choose carefully here if you are listing these categories. Relevancy to your job target and to characteristics needed by a successful person in the occupation counts. Hobbies and awards that showcase your value, and further differentiate you and your personal brand in a positive way from your competition can often be the tipping point in your favor. Unfortunately, Merle's choices demonstrated her high risk-taking nature and were not necessarily a good match for a position that requires stability and common sense.

▷ **Reasons for Leaving:** It is best to leave this for the formal application form; if it is not asked for on the application form, do not include it.

▷ **Salary History:** This information is not needed in a résumé. It may be required on an application form, but even then think twice before divulging this information. Salary history and salary requirements are most often used by employment reviewers as factors to screen you out of consideration, whether your salary is too high (*"we can't afford you"*) or too low (*"why aren't you worth more?"*).

▷ **References:** Although references used to be listed on résumés (perhaps 20 years ago), it is no longer the norm. It breaches the references' confidentiality and could result in identity theft. If the résumé is broadcast too widely and indiscriminately, the references listed could get "burned out" with calls from companies before you have even been invited to an interview. Provide a separate "Reference Data Sheet" (prepared on the same stationery as the résumé) at the time of an interview. Do so only if it is requested, and if you feel there is a good fit between you and the job/company. You will likely need about five references unless you are a senior-level candidate, in which case more will be expected. If you have "juicy tidbits"(one- to two-sentence testimonials), you may want to incorporate them in the Summary section of your résumé that serves as the overview, or perhaps in a pullout sidebar for a more creative approach. Keep in mind that more traditionally conservative industries (such as banking and accounting) may not appreciate a creative approach to your résumé; other industries (such as the arts and entertainment) will find it highly relevant.

Creating a résumé that is a marketing document means you need to hit the nail on the head with up-to-date and appropriate information that proves your skills, industry knowledge and credentials, accomplishments, and value. Anything else in your résumé is the Styrofoam peanuts in a packing box: just pure fluff! Depending on what you chose to include, it may even be downright dangerous to your career life!

Caution: Résumé Typos Ahead!

Job Seeker's Story

With a background in computer science and networking technology, Douglas was confident his résumé would open doors for him. He had hastily prepared a one-page résumé after a recruiter contacted him in need of a Network Engineer with Cisco IOS and Intrusion Detection software experience. Doug e-mailed it to the recruiter in eager anticipation of the conversation that would follow. At the top of the résumé Douglas highlighted *"Network Engineer with Crisco and Contusion Detection experience."*

Charles, a recently laid-off manufacturing engineer, posted his résumé on Monster.com and Careerbuilder.com six months earlier, but was only contacted about sales jobs, which were not his job target. In the Summary section of his résumé, Charles had emphasized required keywords for his desired position, industry, and functions. These keywords included: *Industial Engineering, silicon medicine producks, regulatory complance, resource alocation,* and *team ledership.*

Needing a powerful introductory statement for her pharmaceutical-sales résumé, Sherry highlighted her experience in *"medical transition"* (she meant *"medical transcription"*) and *"vetinary product sales."* Sherry did have a unique and attractive background for pharmaceutical sales, but her rampant typos and grammar mistakes throughout her résumé convinced the employment reviewer that she simply could not communicate well. This was seen as a fatal flaw in her candidacy.

As with Sherry, Kenneth's résumé and cover letter were rife with misspellings and incorrect grammar. As an Editorial Assistant, hoping to move up the food chain to Editor at a large professional association, Kenneth had never been told the real reason for his being "let go": The Editor-in-Charge could no longer tolerate having to correct Kenneth's copy for every weekly newsletter. It was just too much work! Consequently, Kenneth continued to rely on job-search documents that were plagued with grammatical and spelling errors. When Kenneth finally consulted with a professional résumé writer for advice, she counted no less than 35 typos and grammar mistakes in his one-page résumé!

Job Seeker's Stumble

These job seekers are all guilty of résumé slaughter and subsequent interview inactivity due to the most-often-cited reason employment reviewers give for dismissing a résumé: typos and grammatical mistakes. In fact, according to a 2006 survey by OfficeTeam, a leading staffing service, 84 percent of hiring executives indicated they would eliminate a candidate from consideration for two typos; 47 percent said they would do so for only one typo!

Job Seeker's ≥New Strategy≤

Your résumé is the first opportunity you have to make a stellar first impression. There really are only two other options: make no impression at all by not being distinctive in any way from your competition, or stand out by making a horrible first impression. Neither of these two options will garner job interviews.

Whether due to ignorance, laziness, or hastiness, résumé mistakes are the entry point for elimination, and, unfortunately, too many job seekers do not make it past that point. So, what can you do? The obvious spell-check and grammar-check tools in your word-processing software are there to be used, but do not rely on them alone. Proofread your résumé carefully line by line; in fact, you may want to read it line-by-line backwards first just to catch spelling and grammatical errors. Then read it again in normal order to evaluate how the wording flows from one sentence to another. It does matter that you make sense!

Ask friends, family members, or professional colleagues whom you can trust to read and honestly comment on your résumé as well. Not only will they help you in detecting typos and grammar "land mines" in your résumé, but they can also provide valuable feedback regarding wording and sentence structure, completeness of expression, clarity of ideas, gaps of information, and impact of your wording (or lack thereof). You will likely be astounded that what you thought to be a "perfect" résumé is actually laden with mistakes needing correction. Be wise: Do not omit the proofreading step. To do so means your résumé—and job search—are at peril.

One last note: Turn off the grammar-check and spell-check feature in your word processing software after you have successfully completed the proofreading and correction step. Because a résumé is written typically with fragmented phrases, rather than full sentences, you will want to eliminate the green and red wavy lines that will undoubtedly appear throughout your document. This is a reader-friendly step and is a clear signal to the reviewer that you are socially aware of others and show consideration.

Oh, the Tangled Web We Weave...

Job Seeker's Story

Jim had held positions as a Recruiter in six different staffing companies over a nine-year period. That period of time also contained some gaps (up to eight months) when he was unemployed. To camouflage those gaps, Jim changed the dates of his employment on his résumé. He did not want to appear to be a job hopper, and also wanted to appear to be "in demand." Jim asked his good friend Emery, who also happened to be his last employer and CEO of the recruitment firm, to "cover" for him by telling prospective employers that he worked at the company longer than he actually had, and to falsify company records to substantiate that information. Emery reluctantly agreed, although he wasn't sure how he would convince Margaret, the human resources manager, to go along with the scheme. He wasn't even sure he could consistently remember the new dates when called for a reference check by a prospective employer. Emery's concerns were well founded; Jim's falsified employment status was revealed when Margaret refused to validate the incorrect dates of employment.

Another job seeker, Larry, decided to eliminate three of the nine jobs he had held as a security guard in the past 15 years from his résumé. His reasoning seemed flawless: The three jobs had each lasted less than one year, and he had been fired from them. Because he did not want this negative information on his résumé, Larry felt justified in completely eliminating mention of the jobs. Unfortunately, each prospective employer quickly cut Larry from consideration after determining via routine background checks that he had misstated the extent of his employment in the past 15 years on both his résumé and application form.

Sarah, formerly a dental technician, had fabricated both her degree and licensure in Radiological Technology on her résumé to obtain a much-better-paying job. After moving to her new place of employment, more than 250 miles from her previous job, Sarah was fired within three months for falsifying her credentials. She was forced to begin her job search anew, but quickly discovered the word had gotten out about her résumé lies. Sarah was effectively "blackballed" from further employment in the healthcare field in her home state.

Job Seeker's Stumble

These job seekers are fabricating and/or hiding career information on their résumés to favorably impress employment reviewers and secure jobs. Similarly, high-profile careerists, such as university and government officials, have made headlines due to career fraud. Lying on résumés for a variety of reasons is apparently epidemic. According to a 2006 survey by the Society of Human Resource Managers, more than 53 percent of all job applicants lie on their résumés. When asked if they would lie on their résumé to land a job, more than 70 percent of college students said they would. These statistics are well-known by recruiters and hiring authorities, who have felt increasingly compelled to investigate candidates prior to job interviews, before making a job offer, and even after employment. Verifying crucial information, including degrees and licenses held, jobs held and accompanying dates, position titles, and references named, has become a high-growth industry with critical stakes.

Job Seeker's ≳New Strategy≲

Each of the job seekers in these stories could have handled his or her perceived résumé problems in other ways that would have maintained his or her honesty and ensured consideration based on the true facts. Let's review each situation to determine alternative courses of action:

▷ **Employment Gaps:** It is not unusual anymore to be unemployed and seeking employment for several months, or even a year or more. The standard rule is one month of unemployment for every $10,000 of salary—and that's in "normal" economic times. In recessionary periods it will likely be longer. If that's the case, you can explain the "missing" period of time with descriptions such as *"sabbatical for personal/career growth and targeted job search campaign"* or *"family leave combined with career exploration."* Another technique is to use years, rather than months and years, for beginning and end dates of employment.

▷ **Omitting Jobs:** Larry could have focused on the past 10 years on his résumé in which his most recent four jobs had been solid, lasting two to three years each. By building up this segment of his résumé, his final entry of one six-month job held 10 years ago (which ended in his firing) could have been listed as a one- to two-line entry, and thus would have been downplayed. The other "negative" jobs had happened between 11 and 15 years ago, a time frame he could have encapsulated in an overall statement such as, *"security professional for four employers in corporations and government agencies."*

▷ **Falsified Credentials:** Sarah believed it was necessary to do whatever it takes (lying) to get what she felt she deserved: a good-paying job. If Sarah had taken that energy and determination to pursue studies as a Radiological Technician, she could have attained the job of her dreams honestly and had an unbroken pathway to a solid career future. Instead, Sarah's shortcut to credentials not only backfired in losing her job, but it stained her reputation for future employment prospects.

Think about this: Do you want to be flying on a commercial jet when the air traffic controller at your destination airport has lied about his qualifying training, experience, or track record of "near-miss incidents"?

Just Another Boring Job Description

Job Seeker's Story

Josephine felt she was effective in writing her job descriptions for her résumé. She began each one with a paragraph that started with *"Responsibilities included,"* and described what responsibilities she held in the role. These paragraphs could be anywhere from 10 to 20 lines long. She then followed the overview paragraphs with one or two well-written bullets that emphasized a few top results she had achieved in each position. She felt that these few highlights would be enough to show an employer that she was results-driven, and would give a basis for her to talk about all her other achievements in an interview.

When Josephine submitted her résumé for consideration, she could not understand why she was not getting many responses. She had responded to at least 100 job opportunities but had received hardly any calls. Josephine felt the résumé was a strong representation of her skills and achievements, so she was frustrated and stumped about her lack of positive responses.

Job Seeker's Stumble

Josephine had fallen into an easy trap when she created her résumé, which was including responsibility content that was too passive and was not capturing the interest of Human Resources résumé reviewers. When a reviewer first looked at Josephine's most recent position, he or she saw what every candidate who was qualified for the job would have: the same description of passive responsibilities. Therefore, the reviewer began skimming and skipping ahead, saw more responsibilities than results, and moved on quickly, missing much of what Josephine needed her to see.

Job Seeker's ⋛New Strategy⋚

In order to engage reviewers with a dynamic start to each position on your résumé, you must rethink how you begin each position. Specifically, there are actually two key mistakes that job seekers make in stifling the value of their descriptions.

The first is what Josephine did with her starting paragraph that focused on passive responsibilities. Though that seems necessary, it is not the best way to present responsibilities. You should always remember that responsibilities, although needed, do nothing but show that you are equal to other candidates who held similar positions. Being equal is not enough, because reviewers will typically pick a handful of candidates who stand out for excelling at performing those tasks!

The second mistake is avoiding any type of an overview in the job description and jumping directly into a list of bullets. The problem here is that the reviewer is going to have to look at every bullet to really gain a sense of what the position entails. This means he or she will be rapidly skimming and skipping around, most likely missing a lot of the benchmarks that should have captured her attention and positioned you as a strong candidate.

To be most effective and engaging in your job descriptions, you need to take the reviewer by the hand and lead him or her into each position. You will do this by recognizing that you do need a paragraph that acts as connective tissue to take the reviewer from "Here is my title and the company I worked with" to "Here is what I did and how well I did that." That connective piece between those two areas will strengthen the value of the bullets by setting the stage with the challenges and the goals of the position.

For instance, perhaps Josephine was a retail manager. Her old job description started with a responsibility paragraph and followed up with responsibility and achievement-focused bullets. Although her accomplishments sounded good, they were getting lost after the heavy starting paragraph and were not showing the reviewer the major challenges Josephine had faced in attaining them. In reality, Josephine had been recruited after it was found that the prior manager had been skimming funds, an internal theft ring was depleting stock, staff turnover was high, morale was low due to lack of strong leadership, customer service was poor, and sales had been running in the red for the past nine consecutive months.

If Josephine were to capitalize on this information and create a new start to her job description, it might read, *"Recruited to retail operation in order to spearhead a top-to-bottom turnaround, encompassing challenges in financial controls, inventory shrinkage and management, low staff morale and high turnover, poor customer service, and decreasing business resulting in a nine-month revenue slump representing increasing profit decline and significant financial loss. Directed all facets of the turnaround to successfully stabilize operations, achieve profits within three months, and attain continued growth of 10–22% in profit attainment for the past 16 months based on improvements in all areas."*

You can see the difference that starting a position with this energy-packed focus will attain over a passive *"Responsible for"* paragraph or making the mistake of skipping the step altogether and jumping straight into the bullets. Even if you did not have as big of a challenge as Josephine, or had no challenge at all, you can still take advantage of this strategy. Ask yourself: *"What was the goal I was tasked with in this position?"* and *"What challenges did I face in this position?"* You might need to brainstorm, but here are a few of the issues, big and small, that you might capitalize upon:

▷ Did you take over a major project?

▷ Did you find ways to save money?

▷ Were you always seeking to find ways to make operations leaner?

▷ Were you working with a smaller-than-average budget or an incredibly small staff for the level of responsibility?

▷ Were you taking over a department that had problems or replacing an absent boss?

▷ Were you told that this organization was entrenched and successful, and you needed to maintain the status quo, but you still managed to make it more successful?

▷ Did you just find that things were disorganized and you made them better?

▷ Did you start up a new company, division, or department?

▷ Were you tasked with doing something that had not previously been done?

After you have determined your challenge, a few dynamic ways to present this content in a starting paragraph include: *"Challenged to...," "Recruited to...," "Championed the...," "Joined organization with the goal of...,"* or *"Tasked with...."*

Once you set the stage with this short introductory paragraph, you can move into bullets that combine responsibilities with achievements to show the reviewer what you were doing, how you overcame the challenges/met the goals, and what specific results were obtained.

Create a W-I-I-F-M Résumé

Job Seeker's Story

Bradley loved fishing and hunting, and had managed to secure a job right out of college for a top-brand fishing rod manufacturer and distributor. With a bachelor's degree in communications, his love of the outdoors, and an outgoing personality, Brad fit the role of Field Sales Representative very well. After five years of trying to move up the ranks in this family-owned business, Brad realized his career was stalled. Even after talking with the owner of the company about his concerns, Brad did not receive any reassurances about his future with the company.

Thus, Brad began a job search for another Field Sales role that would make the most of his sales background in the outdoor sports industry. He was quickly approached by contacts in the industry who were anxious to have him submit his résumé.

Brad hurriedly wrote his one-page résumé over a weekend, highlighting his job history and duties with bullet points such as *"Responsible for identifying and developing new accounts."* In fact, Brad began every bullet point with *"Responsible for...,"* followed by a specific job duty pulled from his job description.

As Brad distributed his résumé to his eager contacts in the industry, he anticipated a couple of quick interviews and job offers within the month. Sadly, those interviews and job offers did not materialize; in fact, Brad did not hear back from his contacts at all. After leaving them voice-mail and e-mail messages with no response, Brad was discouraged and angry. He felt betrayed. *"After all,"* he thought, *"I supplied my résumé as my contacts requested."* Brad could not fathom why they weren't following up with him.

Job Seeker's Stumble

Brad was well-liked in his industry, so when his professional colleagues heard he was "available," they were intrigued and eager to review his résumé. In the sales world, this situation would be tantamount to having a "warm" lead, which is highly desirable. However, Brad killed his chances with this audience by producing a mundane and ordinary résumé with no proof of value and no personal branding to differentiate him from other candidates. His résumé failed to get buy-in from his industry contacts. In essence, he failed to answer the prospective employer's question: What's in it for me (W-I-I-F-M)?

Job Seeker's ≳New Strategy≲

Although a résumé based on a job description and "responsible for" statements may orient the reviewer to the job duties you have handled, such a résumé does not market you to your target audience. Instead, it positions you as a commodity, the same as many other candidates who possess similar skills and have similar job descriptions. To establish your uniqueness and gain consideration, use the following C-C-A-R formula for each position you have held:

▷ **Context:** As would an artist preparing a blank canvas with white paint before painting a scene on it, prepare the reviewer with the background for your accomplishments to follow. Typical elements to consider include the niche industry, its ranking compared to competitors, the way you were brought on board (if selective and prestigious), who you reported to (if senior management or board of directors), and the scope of your responsibilities (number and type of employees supervised, primary functional duties, and budgeting/profit and loss oversight). This description provides a context for the impressiveness of your accomplishments.

▷ **Challenge:** Explain the problem or challenge you stepped into when you were hired. What did you have to deal with that made your accomplishments even more remarkable? Was the company undergoing a change? What was it? Were you given a turnaround, business-building, client-loyalty revitalization, or new technology transition mission? Was the previous person in your position so outstanding that it was difficult to fill her shoes?

ᐅ **Actions:** Choose the primary skills and actions you took to show how you managed to meet the challenges you faced. These primary actions and how you did them define your personal brand or *modus operandi.* This is the essential piece that allows the reviewer to begin to understand if you could be a company-culture and team-culture match.

ᐅ **Results:** Start your accomplishments bullet points with the results you obtained from the sum of the actions you took over a period of time. Results are directly related to your duties and responsibilities; they represent "what happened" when you performed your job duties and responsibilities. Not every job duty has an exemplary result or is relevant to your job target, so be selective about which ones you want to emphasize in your résumé. Also, the results must be germane to the employer's needs and the accompanying W-I-I-F-M concept.

Quantify the results wherever possible to paint a clearer picture of the scope and impressiveness of your accomplishments. For example, compare these two statements:

Contributed to profits by saving downtime costs on manufacturing production line.

Secured $8 million in manufacturing production-line cost savings over 10 years by reducing downtime by 160 hours annually (average) where per minute labor and materials costs exceeded $100 per minute.

Which of these two statements (both true) has the more powerful impact and more precisely conveys value? By casting a critical eye on your accomplishments you can use both selectivity (to choose the most relevant accomplishments) and quantifiers (to denote the impressiveness of the accomplishments) to flesh out your résumé with W-I-I-F-M results that will catch the reviewer's attention.

Putting the pieces of the C-C-A-R formula together could have yielded this more-compelling résumé content for Brad:

Context and Challenge

Recruited by #3-ranked outdoor sports-equipment company to boost business development and sales in challenging transition to online marketing and sales automation. Within six months of hire, entrusted with managing $250,000 sales department budget and reported to company owner. Selectively hired, trained, and motivated sales team of four field sales reps.

Actions and Results

Revitalized stalled business sales from $300,000 to $800,000 annually, and increased new accounts by 50% within first year by successfully pursuing and capturing overlooked market segments and optimizing newly installed automated sales technology.

Using the C-C-A-R formula allows you to structure your résumé with a consistent pattern of high-value benefits to the prospective employer, answering his W-I-I-F-M question. In addition, it can serve as a vehicle to convey a sense of your personal branding and preferred methods. Because the results and actions taken are bulleted, the reviewer's eye naturally falls on the bullets first when scanning the résumé—and that's exactly what you want. Even if the reviewer plans on only spending 10–30 seconds on your résumé, using this format ensures the key takeaways (prime benefits to the employer) garner immediate favorable notice, so you can be screened in, rather than screened out.

Drowning in a Sea of Résumé Content

Job Seeker's Story

As an Executive Director of a non-profit, Barbara had spent many hours writing her résumé in order to capture exactly what responsibilities she held and what contributions she had made in each position.

The first page of her new two-page résumé included her contact information and then her current position, which she had held for the past five years. This description included 19 bullets, ranging from one line to up to five lines each. Each bullet described a responsibility and started with a past-tense verb.

The second page of her résumé included her early positions, which she had presented in long paragraphs to make all four fit on the page. The page ended with her education, which listed dates the degrees were awarded, followed by school names, and then the actual degree.

When company reviewers in Human Resources would receive Barbara's résumé they would feel overwhelmed by the seemingly endless, unbroken, and heavy list of bullets. They would try to read the document and give her a fair shot, but, because they had hundreds of other applicants, after about 30 seconds of scanning nothing would have stood out or captured their interest. So they would typically move on to a résumé that was easier and quicker to review.

Job Seeker's Stumble

Barbara did not recognize that company reviewers can receive hundreds and even thousands of résumés, both unsolicited (by job seekers who just want to join the company) and solicited (by job seekers who are responding to a specific job posting). Because of this, most résumé reviewers will spend an average of 30 seconds looking to be grabbed by relevant content in a résumé. When these reviewers are met by lengthy, heavy, or thick content in the résumé, the review process can feel quite arduous, and busy reviewers will typically skip and skim, missing much of what the job seeker might have had to offer. In fact, even if reviewers were to have all the time in the world, such a résumé would still put them to sleep.

To increase her chances of success, Barbara should have taken the time to make sure the content in her résumé was bite-sized (quickly readable and scannable) and presented to be sticky and visually distinctive (engaging content that is eye catching).

Job Seeker's ≥New Strategy≤

You are probably asking, *"What does it mean to be bite-sized, sticky, and visually distinctive?"*

▷ **Bite-Sized:** This is content that is written in small, easily scannable pieces, or bits and bytes. With bite-sized information in a résumé you will not find paragraphs longer than four or five lines. In fact, the only place you will find these short paragraphs are in the Summary section at the top of the résumé and at the start of each position to engage the reviewer with a short overview of the position's goals or challenges.

Additionally, bite-sized content never has a bulleted list that is not broken down into shorter, more visually distinctive and sticky sections.

▷ **Sticky and Visually Distinctive:** This is content that is presented in a manner that draws the eye to individual information by using visually distinctive techniques, such as using functional categories to break up a long list of bullets under a single job, or by introducing titles at the beginning of each bullet to define the individual bullets within the list.

For instance, if you have 15 bullets within a job description, you might use either the functional or the title strategy.

Functional Strategy: Using the functional strategy, you would separate the job description/achievement bullets into categories. An Executive Director such as Barbara might break her bullets into small functional categories, such as *Operations & Finance, Marketing & Development, Staffing & HR,* and *Project/Program Management.*

With this strategy, a reviewer will look at the job, and, instead of seeing a long line of bullets or a thick paragraph, his eye will easily be drawn to the category titles.

Titled Bullet Strategy: Using the titled bullet strategy, you would look at the content of the bullet and provide it with a title that represents it appropriately. For example, one of Barbara's bullets would have been about public relations and dealing with the media. Therefore, her bullet would look this way:

- ***Media Relations:*** Interfaced with local and national media to represent....

In this manner, you would provide titles for each bullet, making it very easy for a reviewer to skim down the résumé in seconds to find exactly what experience he is seeking. This is a very powerful technique that makes all your résumé content sticky because no bullet gets lost as one among many in a category or under a job description.

To succeed in making content bite-sized, sticky, and visually distinctive, you should also:

> Focus on leaving a little white space between bullets to further break up the content.

> Use large, clean fonts for text, such as Arial 10 or Times 11, to make content easy to read/review.

> Enhance page presentation by maintaining a clean border of white space around the document with top/bottom margins between .6 and 1 inch, and left/right margins between .8 and 1 inch.

> Rewrite/break up paragraphs that are more than four or five lines long, bullets that exceed three lines each, or lists of more than three bullets.

When content in your résumé is clean, clear, and full of sticky, bite-sized visual cues, you will make it easy for the reviewer to engage with your document!

Providing Clear Direction Regarding Job Targets

Job Seeker's Story

Jeremy did not want to limit his job options, so he did not include an objective at the beginning of his résumé. Therefore, he started his résumé with his Education section followed by his Employment History section.

Stacey wanted to make sure she would be happy with the environment and have opportunities for growth, so she wrote:

Objective: To pursue a position in an organization that embraces teamwork and provides opportunities for growth and advancement based on job performance.

Anthony wanted to show how clever he was, so he wrote an objective sure to get attention:

Objective: To attain the apex of professionalism in low cost mkg, well-disciplined processes in a dynamic and avant grade company, where acquired skills and exp are utilized toward diverse job responsibilities, continued growth and advancement.

Billie had a number of interests, so she wrote an objective that said:

Objective: I am seeking an opportunity that can take advantage of my experience for pharmaceutical or technical sales or my new degree for mechanical/electrical/chemical engineering. I am also open to administrative positions.

Job Seeker's Stumble

Yikes! All four of these candidates have ineffectively, and, in some cases dangerously, used (or not used) the résumé section called the Objective. These mistakes include:

▷ **No Objective (Jeremy):** By leaving off the objective, Jeremy forced the reviewer to look first at his education (first section on the résumé), and then to look at his employment history to get an idea of what type of position he was seeking. This wastes precious review time and may not even be what Jeremy wants to do at this point in his career. Unfortunately, Jeremy did not help the reviewer to see him any other way.

▷ **Selfish Focus (Stacey):** By focusing on what she was seeking in the environment, Stacey forced the reviewer to waste time trying to figure out her job target. She demonstrated that she was, in fact, not targeting companies who were a good match, but just applying anywhere, expecting the company to decide. She did not realize that employers expect you to know in advance and apply correctly, and not passively expect the employer to do it for you.

▷ **Abbreviations, Errors, and Elitism (Anthony):** Anthony tried hard to be catchy, but he ended up ineffectual, incomplete, too long, and unclear.

▷ **Indecision and Lack of Targeting (Billie):** By covering such a diversity of roles ranging from medical sales to IT sales to three types of engineering (based on her degree), Billie pointed out that she did not know what she wanted to do. From an employment reviewer's perspective, Billie might be considered a poor candidate because she could be a flight risk to leave if one of the other opportunities were to arise.

Job Seeker's ≳New Strategy≲

Regardless of the situation, the strategy is the same:

> Always include an Objective (career focus).

> Target the type of position you are seeking, and make certain that you are only pursuing one type of position in a résumé.

> Avoid selfish, self-serving content in the objective.

> Strive for clear, direct content that is short and to the point. You will have the chance to share your strengths and skills in the Summary and Keyword sections below.

> Check carefully for typographical errors in spelling, grammar, and run-on sentences.

When creating an Objective you might use a Header or a traditional Objective. A Header consists of just the title of the type of position you are seeking. For example:

DIRECTOR OF MARKETING.

This will look best if it is centered, bolded, capitalized, and placed in a larger font size, such as 14 or 15 point.

Alternatively, a more traditional Objective would look this way:

Objective: To pursue a position as a Director of Marketing.

You most likely will notice that these examples are very specific to one particular job title. Because you will want to personalize and target your résumé to each position you apply for, the objective should change (along with how the rest of the résumé content is focused) in order to help busy reviewers see a match with their open position in your résumé.

Keep the Audience in Mind When Writing Content

Job Seeker's Story

Marie, a Project Manager, created a résumé that she believed would really tell a reviewer about the projects she had been involved in during her time with her last employer. For example, three of her bullets read:

- Led the ABC project as part of the *Jump and Go* initiative, which was a major success, progressing seamlessly to the delight of all key stakeholders.

- Coordinated the $30M "*Jump and Go*" project— an initiative to migrate AS400 servers to a two-tier redundant environment aided through the development of automated Javascripts that transitioned to server one in a domino effect and later filtered reports for use by programmers who utilized UAT to ensure an optimum go-live experience in the local offices.

- Gained peer distinction by qualifying for the NAR following successful participation in Omega. Recognized by Managing Director for consistently delivering RARs that surpassed all expectations for ROI. Received a Galleon Start for contributions.

She saw these bullets as full of detail and telling a story of exactly what her responsibilities and contribution to the projects entailed. However, when she submitted her résumé to numerous employers she had very few responses. In fact, it seemed her responses were all companies who worked on the contracts with her company and were familiar with the specific projects.

Job Seeker's Stumble

Each one of Marie's bullets represents a different challenge:

The first bullet assumes the reviewer of the résumé is intimately familiar with her project already and understands it fully. It actually says very little and leaves the reviewer wondering what successes were achieved, what was the *Jump and Go* initiative, what progressed seamlessly, what were the results, and who was happy, and why? This is why her only employer responses came from companies who had been involved in the projects.

The second bullet equally assumes the reviewer is familiar with both the project and the overwhelming array of technospeak that follows. Marie has made the mistake of expecting that the first person to review her résumé will be a technology guru who is familiar with her projects and the company's operations. In truth, it will most likely be an individual who has been given brief information by the employer to search out some keywords and phrases, and identify information that communicates the job seeker's achievements and experience.

The third bullet neglects the fact that acronyms will most likely be unfamiliar to many reviewers skimming the résumé, especially if they are unique to the company where they were utilized. In fact, acronyms that are not defined just create stumbling blocks for reviewers. Marie lost the reviewer's attention by providing impenetrable and unclear content.

Job Seeker's ≥New Strategy≤

In order to avoid making similar mistakes, there are a few steps to take that specifically emphasize the importance of separating ego from the résumé writing process. When you get caught up in assumptions about what reviewers will know and understand, you frequently just end up confusing them. Instead, you need to make sure that your content will make sense and cross the bridge to your reviewers' understanding. You can do this by:

▷ Assuming reviewers know nothing about you, what you do, why what you do is important, and how your achievements have made a difference to your current and past employers' prosperity or operation.

▷ Anticipating reviewers' needs and eliminating cloudy or dull information in favor of facts that relate to your experience and how you made the workplace a better place in which to work.

▷ Expecting that, even if you know the acronyms that your industry or company uses, your reviewers may not. It is always a great idea to spell the acronym out the first time it is used.

Utilizing these strategies, here's how a rewrite of Marie's three bullet points might look:

- Eliminated network congestion, improved staff productivity, and transformed standard management reports into informative decision-making tools by leading a team of six on the $30M Jump and Go initiative.

- Designed a simple, yet effective infrastructure, troubleshot and resolved numerous issues surrounding incompatible hardware and software, and delivered the Jump and Go project within the three-month deadline and meeting budget forecasts.

- Won acceptance to company's prestigious National Assessment Program (NAP) for Managers—an elite succession planning initiative rewarding the state's top two managers.

- Successfully completed company's benchmark customer service program Omega, in tandem with gaining recognition for pinpointing asset volume anomalies, which prompted Managing Director's public praise to surpassing goals.

When you articulate your strengths and achievements in a meaningful way, you provide reviewers with a door that opens into your world. Take the time to make sure you communicate information clearly and concisely to help reviewers see your value.

Grab Attention With a Keyword Summary

Job Seeker's Story

Anthony, a top-level sales and marketing Account Executive, had been in the job-search mode for the past year as he saw his start-up entrepreneurial venture struggling in a tight economy. Finally, as Anthony's resources began to seriously diminish, he put in a concentrated effort to get back into corporate account management by updating his résumé. After he had listed his past job history, dates of employment, and education, Anthony included the following Objective statement at the top of his one-page résumé:

Objective: A challenging and rewarding position that will maximize my experience in sales and marketing.

After six months of distributing this résumé for job openings both online and offline, Anthony had not received one request for an interview.

Job Seeker's Stumble

Although Anthony's résumé needed improvement in many respects, he had failed to garner initial attention from an employment reviewer by wasting prime résumé "real estate" (the top half of his one-page résumé). Instead, he chose to lead his résumé with a clear indicator of what he expected from the hiring company, not what he could do for the company. Unfortunately, this type of bland and banal Objective statement is quite commonplace and does nothing to positively impact anyone's candidacy. In fact, Anthony's "first impression" is both self-serving and unimaginative, two traits that did not endear him to prospective employers or recruiters.

Job Seeker's New Strategy

As a marketing tool, your résumé's first order of business is to grab the attention of the reviewer in a positive manner and highlight your value to the company. It is not about what you want out of a company. With years of great experience, Anthony could have started off his résumé with a powerful Summary section, rather than an Objective. The Summary section, in particular, can be an immediate "clincher" in evoking interest if it is done well. The following components are critical to writing such a well-done Summary:

▷ **Value Proposition:** Your value proposition must connect with the reviewer's concept of what constitutes an ideal candidate for a particular job. It needs to go beyond simply relaying skills via a job-description excerpt. Instead, your value proposition needs to acknowledge the benefits the employer is seeking, which ultimately revolve around the bottom line (for example, how much money generated and/ or how much money saved). Showing how you have a track record of delivering those benefits in previous jobs serves to segue the reviewer from the benefits employers' want to the thought that you could be the candidate to provide those very same benefits. Providing brief tidbits of proof—similar to "dangling the bait" when fishing—entices the reviewer to read beyond the Summary section and into the body of your résumé, where more substantiating evidence of your value resides in terms of quantifiable accomplishments.

Therefore, Anthony's Summary paragraph could have started with:

"Top-Tier Account Manager in medical device industry with award-winning strengths in new business development, sales, and customer relationship management. Track record of $350 million to $500 million in revenue generation for the past three years and 10% year-over-year profit gains."

▷ **Personal Brand:** Your value proposition tells *what* you can deliver to your prospective employer; your personal brand combines that concept with *how* you do it. That's what makes personal branding so "personal": It is a reflection of the uniqueness within each and every one of us. Sometimes called a "Unique Selling Proposition" (USP), a personal brand can also be shortened into a tagline or slogan.

Developing a slogan or tagline can only come after you discover your personal brand. Your personal brand is about authenticity and what is real about you; it is not about "creating" a brand out of thin air or developing a marketing pitch in a vacuum. Even marketers know to conduct focus groups of consumers who can give realistic feedback so that brand attributes and a slogan can emerge. In a similar fashion, Anthony could get feedback about his brand via an informal survey of people who know him well. Or he could use the 360Reach assessment, an online personal branding assessment from the Reach Branding Club (*www.reachbrandingclub.com*).

An example slogan for Anthony that reflects his personal brand, based on both the sales results he has achieved in the past and his personal style of delivery could have read, *"Consistent multi-million-dollar sales results as the clients' #1 go-to person."*

▷ **Keywords:** Keywords are usually nouns and noun phrases, and are the current occupation and industry terminologies, similar to "buzzwords." To be certain you are including these up-to-date keywords in your résumé, do an online search for at least 10 job postings in your occupational field and level, such as "Account Executive." Make note of the number of times specific keywords appear in the job posting, especially the job description and the requirements areas. Then sort these keywords into *required* and *desired* categories. Required keywords are those that appear in almost every job posting; those must be incorporated into the Summary as well as the body of your résumé. For Anthony's chosen career (Account Executive), *business development, sales, account management,* and *client relationship management* are all required keywords. Desired keywords do not appear quite as often as required keywords; you can be more selective about which ones to use. By top-loading your résumé with these keywords in your Summary, you are providing a sort of Cliff's Notes to the proof of value to follow in your résumé.

Required and desired keywords must reflect your real experience. Do not add keywords to "pad" your résumé if you are not prepared to talk about your experience with those keywords in an interview. Keywords arise naturally from a vast array of possibilities, such as occupations, industries, job titles and levels, skills, strengths, attributes, degrees, schools, training, continuing professional development, work experience, geographic areas, technology skills, language skills, licenses, certifications, professional associations, community involvement, and leadership activities that prospective employers determine are intrinsically related to a particular job. Keywords are the "search string" of words a hiring manager enters into a database program or scans for visually on a résumé to quickly find the best "quality match" candidates.

The Summary section of your résumé is high-powered territory. You can use it to ensure your résumé does not linger in résumé-database limbo. By top-loading the Summary with a value proposition and keywords, you are signaling to the reviewer that you are a candidate to be taken seriously. By going the extra step of incorporating your personal brand, you can etch a memorable image of your signature style that allows the reviewer a glimpse of possible culture fit and leadership potential.

Because the Summary is typically one to two paragraphs followed by a separate Keyword area, it can easily be repurposed for bios and profiles on online social networking sites. This tactic will immediately serve to increase your online visibility for career development and for job search throughout your work span. Consequently, a Summary richly laden with keywords, value, and personal branding can grab attention in both the online and offline worlds via social networking and social media, and job-search collateral materials, such as a résumé, respectively. Premiere visibility is the first step on the road to a job offer. Take that first step with a well-crafted Summary and watch the results pour in.

Stop Looking the Same as Everyone Else and Hurting Scannability

Job Seeker's Story

Thomas had been applying for positions for several months with no response. He was very proud of his résumé, which had been created using a document template, and he felt he had saleable job skills, so could not understand what was wrong.

At a job fair, Thomas spoke with Lily, a professional résumé writer. After looking at his résumé, she picked up several others from a stack on her table and held them up next to his. *"Do you see any difference between these?"* she asked.

Thomas looked at them and said, *"Not really; they look very similar."*

Lily went on to explain to Thomas that he was using the same word-processing résumé template as many other job seekers. She explained that a résumé is supposed to help you stand out from the competition, and when many candidates use the same résumé template, they all end up looking exactly alike.

If an employer were to receive Thomas's current résumé, he would just blend into the applicant pool, something he could not do if he wanted to stand out and get reviewed.

She also explained that the résumé template used tables, which might cause problems if reviewers tried to convert his file to a text document and scan it into their keyword résumé database. Tables might actually cause content to disappear from his résumé. Additionally, she told him that the template format was limiting him through use of a small font, over-emphasis on employment dates, ineffective content order, no summary section, and lack of visual punch.

Job Seeker's Stumble

Thomas was missing the boat with his generic résumé for all the reasons listed: He did not stand out from the competition, his font was tiny, his format was dull, his skills section was forced to the bottom of page two of the résumé, and his dates were over-emphasized as the first item at the start of each new job description. As long as his résumé blended in, he would not stand out.

Job Seeker's ≥New Strategy≤

This one is easy: Never, never, never use a résumé template provided in your word-processing software program to format your final résumé. Although it might be a good starting point for collecting your content, you are going to want to use a much more scannable and unique presentation for your final draft.

Your résumé is a marketing and positioning tool that lets you compete against other candidates for an employment position, so it must present you individually and not look the same as all the rest. It is important to adhere to basic requirements and sections of a résumé. However, the visual presentation and order of content will depend on what is most important, what you need to deemphasize, and how the document looks when you get it laid out.

A few strategies to keep your document scannable and avoid the trap of a generic résumé template include:

▷ Place your name on the top line of the résumé.

▷ Keep margins clean and neat to maintain adequate white space on the page.

▷ Include dates, but not as the first item in the job description or education listings. Dates are usually the last thing you want to emphasize because they waste time in letting reviewers get to a job title match, and can show the job was too short, too long, or too old.

▷ Help reviewers find important information first. For instance, in the Education section, unless the college you attended is more impressive than the degree you obtained, always list the degree first, and bold it. This can also apply to the order of sections in your résumé. A new graduate might put education near the top, whereas a seasoned professional would put it near the end.

▷ Use a font size for body text of Arial 10 or Times 11. Avoid using the default Times 10, as it is too small for easy readability. Header fonts should be larger to help the reviewer rapidly distinguish between sections.

▷ Keep in mind that reviewers naturally read left to right (and OCR scanners do the same), so it is a good idea to lay out your résumé that way. Keep your résumé scannable and readable by avoiding two-column template formats.

▷ Utilize visual techniques such as bolding, italics, and capitalization sparingly to make content stand out. Overuse of these visual strategies can backfire by making the content hard to read.

▷ Exclude optional sections recommended in a template format that do not apply to you or help with your candidacy for the job, such as affiliations, hobbies, or volunteer work.

The only time you should ever use a résumé template is when it is required by the agency you are applying to or the one that is helping you find your new position. Otherwise, you should create a visual, scannable document that makes you stand out from the crowd.

Do You Know What's on Your Résumé?

Job Seeker's Story

Cecilia was anxious about her first interview after six weeks of an unfruitful job search. Most of the résumés she had e-mailed to employers in response to job postings on the Internet had gotten no reply whatsoever. She had a few phone interviews that did not seem to last very long and resulted in no second interviews. Consequently, this upcoming face-to-face interview was really important to her. Besides, she hated doing this job-search stuff anyway, and just wanted another job as a Call Center Representative, similar to the one she had with a big food and beverage company before she was downsized.

The interviewer, David, could see that Cecilia was nervous, but many applicants were nervous. He would not let that deter him from conducting a thorough interview for what he felt was a critical front-line position. That's because the person who served in the Call Center Representative position would be the first point-of-contact with the public and media in responding to inquiries, complaints, and sometimes even crises. David took his responsibility for selecting a candidate for this position very seriously.

The interview began routinely with small talk to break the ice and a brief description of the duties of the applied-for job. Then David turned his attention to Cecilia's résumé and scrutinized the last job she had held as a Call Center Representative.

David asked, *"Your résumé indicates you 'scheduled installations, exchanges, parks buy-backs, and removals of equipment and other assets using information systems, supplier networks, and agent contacts in order to meet customer expectations.' Exactly what does that mean?"*

Cecilia looked bewildered and started to turn red as she responded, *"I thought you would know what that means. I think it means I took phone calls from many different departments and relayed information."*

It was now David's turn to be taken aback. Shaking his head, he asked, *"What do you mean you 'think' it means you took phone calls and relayed information? Don't you know what your résumé is saying?"*

Cecilia blurted out, *"My boss was unhappy about having to lay me off and she helped me with my résumé."*

David dug deeper and asked, *"What exactly did your boss do to help you?"*

Wringing her hands, Cecilia admitted, *"Well, she sort of wrote it for me."*

Although David was incredulous that Cecilia did not understand what her résumé said, he felt he had to ask for clarification: *"Did you ever go over it with her so she could explain what she had written and why she had written it?"*

Cecilia hung her head and said, *"I was embarrassed to ask. It seemed like I should have known without asking her and I was just thankful that she was helping me at all."*

Although David felt sorry for Cecilia, he was also angered that he had wasted his time on this applicant when there were so many others he could have interviewed instead. David did not continue with the planned behavior-based questions and the rest of the interview. He quickly ended the conversation and wished Cecilia good luck in her job search. She was disqualified from further consideration for the Call Center Representative position.

Job Seeker's Stumble

Cecilia's lack of knowledge about her own past, as reflected in her résumé content, left the interviewer disinterested in her as a candidate. Her inability to describe what the job duties listed on her résumé meant showed her lack of common sense in diverse ways: that she did not expect she would have to explain her résumé content in an interview, that she did not ask for clarification of the content from the person who actually wrote her résumé, and that she did not apologize for wasting the interviewer's time.

Job Seeker's ≳New Strategy≲

The solution to this mishap is obvious: Your résumé is about *you*, so you must know what it says and be ready to explain it in an interview. You may need to solicit assistance with writing your résumé, and that's fine. Many times it is difficult to write about ourselves, no matter how well-educated or knowledgeable we may be. Or perhaps your writing talent is not all that great, and it's challenging to find just the right words. That's not unusual. Whether it's a good friend or colleague, or a professional résumé writer, many people turn to others for help with writing and/or editing their résumé.

The caution here is to get involved in the process and understand what your résumé says! Who else is going to defend it in an interview except you? If your friend or a former boss, as in Cecilia's case, wants to insert whole blocks of text from your job description, at the very least understand what that job description is saying. Incidentally, this approach of using parts of your job description verbatim for your résumé is a very simplistic approach, and very boring. So, all in all, this technique, although fairly easy, is not highly successful.

If someone recommends certain keywords be used liberally throughout the résumé, know what those keywords mean both by themselves and in the context of your résumé. For example, if you wrote marketing communications materials and the interviewer asked you about your "marcomm" experience, would you know what he was talking about? You should—and you could then proceed to sell yourself by talking about your marcomm accomplishments!

Market Your Strengths, Not Your Weaknesses

Job Seeker's Story

As an Information Technology (IT) Manager rising through the ranks, Patrick had worked diligently on his job search after being let go from his last company due to a merger and restructuring. He prepared his one-page résumé and submitted it numerous times in response to online job postings where he was certain his skills were a perfect match for the job listed. He was surprised, therefore, when the résumé failed to produce results, especially in instances when he was very well qualified for the advertised position.

Patrick decided to consult with Lance, a professional résumé writer, to shed some light on the lack of responses his résumé was getting. In the analysis that followed, the first thing Lance noticed was that Patrick had used a functional format for his résumé that segmented his job duties into three functional areas: Networking and Systems Administration, Project Management, and Client Relations. Each of these functional areas summed up his relevant job duties at all of his various employers into brief paragraphs with no information on achievements related to each job.

Second, Lance was struck by the fact that Patrick had placed the listing of his jobs at the beginning of the résumé rather than positioning it at the end. This uppermost placement was particularly unfortunate because, out of the six jobs listed in Patrick's seven-year career history, three jobs had lasted six months or less.

When Lance questioned Patrick about his choice of the functional format and his list presentation of jobs first, Patrick replied, *"Well, I have switched jobs frequently and want an employer to know that about me first, so then they can decide whether to interview me after that."*

Job Seeker's Stumble

There are three major blunders in Patrick's résumé, and they are all related to not showcasing his strengths. First, Patrick's rationale that an employer would be eager to assess negative information to determine whether to call him in for an interview *did* produce results, but not the ones he desired. By putting his red flags of working at 50 percent of his jobs (three out of six) for less than six months each in the top one-third of this one-page résumé, Patrick unwittingly and prominently characterized himself as a job hopper. This made it easy for employment reviewers to screen Patrick out of consideration, which is the initial step in the candidate selection process.

Second, Patrick used the functional résumé format—not a particularly good choice for the IT management field where it tends to produce a low rate of return for interviews.

Third, simply summarizing job duties in a brief paragraph for each of three functional areas may be the easiest and quickest way to write a résumé, but does not do much to impress the employment reviewer. After all, wouldn't others who have worked at jobs similar to Patrick have similar job duties? So, what reason would an employer have to select Patrick for an interview over someone else? Patrick had succeeded in compiling a one-two-three knockout combination of reasons in his résumé for being dropped from consideration—100 percent of the time!

Job Seeker's ≥New Strategy≤

Turning around Patrick's "knockout" résumé involved tackling the three major mistakes. The following techniques address each specifically:

▷ **Lead With Your Strengths:** Patrick's focus should have been on using the résumé as an opportunity to present himself in the best possible light. Leading with your "good stuff" allows the employment reviewer to form a positive first impression. Even if the reviewer only scans the résumé quickly, most "eye time" is spent on the top one-third of the résumé. So place your strengths above the fold (the top half of the page).

Your strengths might be your degrees or certifications, either because they are recent (new) or prestigious for your field. Or perhaps your most recent job is the one you were in the longest, and where you had the most significant accomplishments. Maybe you possess unique technology or language skills that are in demand for the job you are pursuing. Any or all of these could be included in a Summary at the top of your résumé or in a categorized section above the fold.

If you have a career history that contains several short-duration jobs, you could certainly use years only, instead of months and years, for the dates of employment. If your job history is longer than 10–15 years, you could condense the earlier work history into one-line entries at the bottom with a category title of "Early Employment," and leave off dates altogether. You may even want to consider omitting early employment, especially if it dates back 20–30 years.

▷ **Choose the Most Marketable Format:** There are three most commonly used résumé formats: reverse chronological (the traditional hands-down favorite of employment reviewers), functional (least appreciated by reviewers), and combination (marriage of both the reverse chronological and functional formats). In Patrick's field of IT management, the reverse chronological format is the most accepted by hiring authorities. By making use of that format, Patrick would have immediately signaled to the reviewer that he understood the conventions of his field for résumé acceptability and was willing to provide his résumé content in that manner.

▷ **Gain Credibility With Accomplishments:** Being the same as every other candidate by listing a rote set of job duties (probably taken directly from a job description) for résumé content is not going to win many interviews. However, standing out positively with powerful accomplishments can be counted on to gain attention and calls. Wouldn't an employer rather hire someone he can depend on to produce valuable results for the organization, rather than someone who is a "seat warmer"?

Do not expect an employment reviewer to read between the lines. Give him clear and compelling achievements, quantifiable measurements of success for past jobs, and he will be able to envision similar results being produced for his company. Be careful not to overstep the bounds of believability. Stretching the truth is never a good practice for your résumé. However, claiming every ounce of real accomplishments is not only desirable; it is a must-do résumé tactic if you want to generate enough calls to land interviews. And interviews are the route to job offers.

After Patrick incorporated these suggestions into his résumé, he called Lance back in 10 days, exclaiming, *"The phone has been ringing non-stop ever since I implemented your suggestions. Thank you for pointing out what should have been obvious to me."* Patrick accepted a new position in IT management shortly thereafter.

Dating Your Experience and Education for Success
Job Seeker's Story

Jade had worked in Maintenance Management during her 33-year career. When Human Resources résumé reviewers first received her résumé they would initially think she had left dates off completely. However, after looking closely, they noticed that at the end of each of her paragraph-style job descriptions she had included entries such as *"Employed 211 months."* It turned out that she had listed the number of months for which she held each position instead of including actual dates.

Harold had been working consistently for the last 21 years. However, he was re-entering a career field in which he had not worked for 10 years. Because he was concerned that much of his relevant experience was dated, he opted to leave dates off his résumé completely.

Shirley, currently a Director of Marketing, included her entire employment chronology, dating back to 1961 and including early internships and administrative positions. This length required that she have a three-page résumé with 13 positions listed and detailed.

Jade, Harold, and Shirley were all equally frustrated in their lack of responses to their résumé submissions and could not understand why.

Job Seeker's Stumble

The problem occurring for each of these three job seekers represents two extremes around the use of dates in the résumé. The bottom line is that leaving dates off immediately raises a red flag that Jade and Harold probably had something negative to hide, such as dated experience, big gaps between jobs representing possible problems in health or responsibility level, or trying to hide their age. Alternatively, listing older dates (1960s, 1970s, and even early 1980s), as Shirley did, gave reviewers more information than they needed, and quite possibly worked against Shirley, based on assumptions that might have been made about her salary requirements or age.

Job Seeker's >New Strategy<

When you are writing a résumé you need to be sensitive to what dates can mean on your résumé. The rule of thumb for dates is:

▷ Always include dates for the last 10–15 years of employment. If you want to or need to include earlier experience, you should include it in a section called "Additional Experience" or "Early Experience." Do not include dates on these earlier roles.

▷ Avoid Jade's mistake of trying to be clever with your dates. Reviewers will see through this and know you are trying to hide something. List years, or months and years, after the job title and company name for each position (again, in the last 10–15 years).

▷ Leave off early jobs altogether that do not position you for your job. It is not necessary to list every job you have ever held, as Shirley did in her résumé. You will end up looking as if you have held too many jobs, wasting valuable space in your résumé, and having dates that may go back too far.

▷ Consider leaving dates off of education/degrees except when required. Dates in the Education section either can show that your learning is too new and unused, or too old and out of date.

Keep these rules in mind and you will not go wrong in dating yourself in your résumé.

Mind the Gaps in Your Employment Time Line
Job Seeker's Story

Elizabeth was a stay-at-home mom for the past six years. Although she had volunteered during that time for a few local organizations, and even performed bookkeeping for her husband's business, she did not think these counted. So she just left a six-year gap in her résumé, and listed her last secretarial position with the ending date of six years before.

Alternatively, Sarah Beth did not want to leave a gap, so she listed, *"Home care to children—2002 to Present."*

Timothy had a stroke and had spent seven years learning to walk, speak, and retrain for his career. He left a seven-year gap in his résumé.

Job Seeker's Stumble

Deciding how to cover gaps in the timeline was a real problem for Elizabeth, Sarah Beth, and Timothy. Each sought to overcome the gap: two by ignoring it and hoping for the best, and one by listing something that could possibly hurt her chances for a job. Each of these techniques would act as a red flag for the reviewer, which could create a solid barrier to a job interview despite how qualified the early career experience might have been.

All three were going to struggle landing interviews until they found ways to successfully deal with their gaps.

Job Seeker's ≳New Strategy≲

First of all, there are typically five types of gaps:

1. Taking time off to be a full-time caregiver to children or elderly parents.

2. Requiring time off to recover from an illness or accident.

3. Taking time off to go back to school full-time.

4. Pursuing time off for some type of sabbatical (to write a book, travel the world, and so forth).

5. Losing months of time due to inability to find a new job after a layoff or downsizing.

Regardless of your situation, you need to address your gap. It can be extremely easy to deal with, as in #3 (going back to school). All you need to do in this situation is to incorporate it into your employment chronology: "*Full-time Student, Business Administration—University of Georgia, Athens, GA—2005 to 2007.*" If this represents a new career field, then you might also include highlights of school projects, papers, and subjects to show reviewers what you now have to offer.

If you have taken time off to be a caregiver to children or parents, then it can be as simple as including the single line "*Home Care to Family Member—Chicago, IL—2002 to 2007*" in your employment chronology. It is not a good idea to mention children, because the employer you are targeting may be influenced based on negative experiences with parents of young children having attendance problems.

If you have been providing care to parents or children while also working, volunteering, or taking career-advancing courses, you might want to alter how you address your gap. For instance, if you volunteered you might put "***Administrative & Fundraising Volunteer**—Yellow Umbrella, Stokes, FL— 2004 to Present*" followed by a description of your contribution, if it is relevant. If you were performing book-keeping for a family business, list this as you would any job: "***Bookkeeper**—Dowling Plumbing, Seattle, WA—2001 to Present*" followed by the description (again, if it is relevant).

Perhaps you were taking time off for a sabbatical. In this case, how you incorporate it into your time line will depend on what you are doing. For instance, if you were also working on a degree, enhancing cultural experience by traveling the world, finishing a manuscript that you are now shopping around for publication, or sitting on a board of directors, any of these items could become listings in your chronology versus simply listing "***Sabbatical**—Greenville, SC—2006 to 2007.*"

If you were not working due to an illness, using the "sabbatical" listing is the best way to go. You will just need to be prepared to provide a positive explanation of how this will not be a barrier to your performance today.

If your gap is due to unemployment, seriously consider how long the gap is before choosing to mention it in your time line. Statistics show that it can take one month of job search for every $10,000 you want to earn. Therefore, multi-month gaps are not uncommon. If your gap is several months or more than a year, you might just shift to listing years only versus months and years in your employment chronology.

Think your way through your gaps to provide a positive and proactive listing in your work chronology so that a reviewer is not left having to figure it out and thinking the worst.

Over-Qualified Can Mean Unemployed

Job Seeker's Story

Bruce had negotiated an incredible compensation package in his last Director of Engineering position, where he had earned a six-figure income, and which had resulted in a three-year paid severance when he was downsized. However, it had now been three years, and, though he had enjoyed the first year and had been consulting for the last two, he was no closer to a job offer despite nine months of consistent job search. In frustration, he sought a career consultant to advise him on what he might be doing wrong.

The career coach, Misha, first looked at his résumé and noticed that he had earned his PhD, and when he introduced himself it was as "Dr. Seivers." She asked Bruce if the positions he applied for ever asked for a doctorate, and he said no. She asked if his bosses typically had doctorates, and he again replied no. She then explained to him that, although a doctorate was truly an impressive achievement and deserved recognition, it was most likely hurting him in his job search. She went on to tell him that if it was not a requirement for the job, he might be deemed as expecting too high of a salary, and if his superiors felt he was more highly educated than they were, they might be intimated.

Bruce was unhappy and a little resistant to the suggestion, but decided to give it a try on a few of his job applications. He removed the doctorate from his otherwise strong résumé, stopped introducing himself as a doctor, resumed his job search, and received an impressive job offer that represented a significant wage increase in less than 30 days.

Job Seeker's Stumble

As would most people, Bruce thought that advances in education would cause him to be perceived as a highly motivated professional focused on life-long learning. That is frequently the case in certain academic, scientific, and medical fields as well as for high-paid consultants and entrepreneurs, but in situations such as Bruce's, it just made him intimidating, potentially over-qualified, and possibly too expensive for prospective employers to consider.

Job Seeker's ≳New Strategy≲

This is another easy fix. Be proud of the accomplishment, but seriously weigh whether it is actually helping or hurting your job search candidacy. If, similar to Bruce, you are over-qualified based on educational requirements or always have a higher degree than the positions one to two levels above your target require, it is probably time to check your ego at the door and remove the degree from your résumé.

Should it be discovered that you have not listed your advanced degree, you can explain that you left it off because it was not relevant to your job target: You pursued the degree for your own personal edification and felt it did not add to your qualifications for the position.

This same approach on disclosure can work on unrelated certifications and licensure (for another career field), early jobs that are several years old and irrelevant to your target, and sensitive items such as inappropriate hobbies.

Although it might feel little painful not to acknowledge your achievements, remember that the résumé is all about target marketing for your desired position. If you are not perceived as over-qualified, you will have a much greater opportunity to land the interview and get the job.

CHAPTER 3

Cover Letter Casualties

^

Beware of Ego Overkill

Job Seeker's Story

With a bachelor's degree in psychology and master's degree in clinical psychology, Carrie had initially gotten a job as a mental health counselor with a large, residential treatment facility for teenagers. She had been there a few years, but was really beginning to miss being back in the Midwest where she grew up, and she was getting bored.

As Carrie broadened her job search to include all types of counseling jobs, she excitedly penned a cover letter for a job posting in Cincinnati, her hometown. She wrote:

> I am writing to you because I want to take this opportunity in my life to relocate back to Cincinnati, the home of my birth. I feel it is time to move back from the East Coast where I got my schooling and am currently employed.
>
> Last week I learned about your opening for a High School Mental Health Counselor while speaking with a friend. I then called someone at the school district office who confirmed the Mental Health Counselor position was still open. I believe my education and experience are just right for this job.

I have included my previous employment background, as well as my phone number and e-mail address, on the attached résumé. I would like the opportunity to talk with you to further discuss the salary and benefits you are offering before I come to Cincinnati to interview. I can be reached on my cell phone—see my résumé for the precise contact information. I look forward to hearing from you by Friday.

As Carrie mailed her résumé and cover letter to Cincinnati on Monday, she started counting the days until Friday when she felt sure she would get a return phone call. Unfortunately, Carrie's hopes were dashed. There was no phone call, only a letter stating that the position had been filled.

Job Seeker's Stumble

This cover letter, while written sincerely, missed the mark. Carrie's overuse of the word "I" to begin almost every sentence, as well as emphasis on her need to find out the salary and benefits first, leaves an impression of being very self-centered and lacking in professional communication skills. With no mention of her actual qualifications, Carrie left it up to the reviewer to find that information on her résumé.

Job Seeker's ≷New Strategies≷

Starting sentences with the word *I* is a commonly seen plague in cover letters. Learning to vary sentence structure is one way to overcome that mistake. Let's deconstruct Carrie's letter to improve her self-marketing content and grammatical flow, and change the tone from self-serving to helpful. Here are a few tips:

▷ **Focus on Their Needs, Not Yours:** It is fine to state that you wish to relocate and why, but that self-centered need should not be cited as the driving force behind your motive to apply for the position. Instead, Carrie could have written:

Emily Warren, the Superintendent at the Plainfield School District, suggested I contact you directly regarding the position of Mental Health Counselor at Plainfield High School, as my qualifications are a perfect match with your requirements. With my professional experience helping teenagers manage mental-heath issues, as well as my familiarity with Plainfield High School (I am a native of Cincinnati), I could acclimate quickly to your school and begin providing immediate mental-health services.

▷ **Build in Highly Visible Proof:** Provide the reviewer with proof of accomplishments in the cover letter and facilitate readability with "sound bites" of information. For example, Carrie could have written:

My strengths and accomplishments are noted in detail on my résumé. Here is just a brief glimpse of what you will find:

- Psychological training in adolescent stressors, addictions counseling, and suicide prevention. Achieved 4.0 GPA in both master's degree and bachelor's degree programs.

- Two years of experience in a residential treatment facility for adolescents (ages 14–19) with mental-health and substance-abuse issues. Voted "Most Valuable Employee" for six (out of eight) consecutive quarters of service.

- Experience with dually diagnosed adolescents. Received commendation for quick thinking in crisis intervention with distraught teenage resident.

- Leadership role model with teenagers. Volunteered in high school after-hours recreation programs and in homeless shelters to intervene with mental-health issues and provide stability and mental-health resources. Recommended by high school principal and director of homeless shelter to other volunteer programs.

▷ **Close With Consideration and Confidence:** Be considerate of the reviewer's time; include your contact information in your cover letter. Carrie might have said:

If the characteristics and accomplishments I have noted describe the candidate you desire, may we talk soon? I am very eager to bring my genuine caring and compassion, combined with my proven mental-health skills, to the students of Plainfield High School. You can reach me on my cell phone at 555-222-3333 during the day. Thank you for your consideration.

In fact, every document you send, whether a résumé, cover letter, bio, references list, thank-you letter, or follow-up letter, should contain your contact information. If your cover letter became separated from your résumé, for example, then you could still be contacted. Showing consideration for the reviewer's time may seem to be a small matter, but it subtly signals a professional approach and team spirit.

Proof, Proof, and Proof Some More

Job Seeker's Story

Darryl had been with the same company for 18 years as an Electrical Engineer when he was laid off. After he got over the initial shock, he began to send out résumés and cover letters in response to online job postings he discovered on Monster and CareerBuilder. Darryl felt fortunate that he lived in a big metropolitan area where the demand for electrical engineers was plentiful. He was sure his job search would be over in a matter of weeks.

Here's one of the cover letters that Darryl penned:

Re: Your electrical enginere position

   I have attained 18 years of experience as a electrical engineer with the Amce manufacturing company. There have never been any complainants about my word and I have always gotten pay raises. I feel that reflects well on my abilities. I do not have any wage stipulations, however I feel that salary could be negotiated consonantly with my experience.

   I consider myself a motivational individual, with a purposeful attitude having the ability to be flaxable and adaptible to any new opportunes with ease and determination.

   Please contact me as soon as possible regarding this postion. Thank you for your time.

Three months later, after having sent out hundreds of résumés accompanied with cover letters similar to this one, Darryl was still searching.

Job Seeker's Stumble

   Although his qualifications were stellar, Darryl had inadvertently harmed his chances of being considered due to two simple mistakes: typographical and grammatical errors.

Job Seeker's ≥New Strategies≤

   Employment reviewers have extremely low tolerance for grammatical errors and typos. In fact, even one error of that nature could be enough to throw your application out of consideration, no matter how well-qualified you are. That may seem unfair, but the reality is reviewers use this initial benchmark routinely to screen out the hundreds (and sometimes thousands) of applicants for a single position. Using clearly defined benchmarks, such as grammar, punctuation, and spelling, makes their job of narrowing the field of candidates much easier. After all, who would want to hire someone who was so careless?

Isn't the quality of the cover letter and résumé a direct indicator of the care that person might give to his or her job?

To avoid being eliminated in the first round due to simple language errors, consider these suggestions:

▷ **Proofread—And Then Do It Again:** It would seem with spell-check that the possibility of typos should be non-existent. However, if your typo results in the creation of a real word, instead of your intended word, that typo will not be flagged. For example, Darryl said, *"There have never been any **complainants** about my **word**,"* when he meant to say, *"There have never been any **complaints** about my **work**."*

In addition, Darryl misspelled the job title for which he was applying (***enginere*** instead of ***engineer***) in the reference line of the letter. This is one of the first things read in the letter. Typos are unacceptable anywhere in the letter, and having a typo occur in such a prominent place virtually ensures your application will be screened out. Altogether, Darryl has a total of 13 grammatical errors and typos in his cover letter of 105 words!

Pay attention to spell-check, but do not rely on it to catch every mistake. Proofread your cover letter by reading it out of order; start with the bottom paragraph, instead of the first. That alone may allow you to pick up mistakes you might not otherwise notice.

▷ **Say It Simply:** If complex language is not your natural style, refrain from using it. Trying to impress reviewers with "big words" can misfire, especially if you are not using them correctly. For example, Darryl said, *"I do not have any wage stipulations, however I feel that salary could be negotiated **consonantly** with my experience."* Obviously, Darryl meant to say *"negotiated **commensurately** with my experience."* Perhaps a more straightforward approach (such as *"I would be happy to discuss salary at the time of* *the interview*") would have been more appropriate and less likely to cause language difficulties.

▷ **Ask Others to Proof:** Whether you consider yourself adept in the English language or not, have someone with a good sense of grammar and spelling check your cover letters. We often do not catch our own mistakes. Unfortunately, all it takes is one to jeopardize your application. If you belong to a job search group or know other job seekers in your network, you could offer to reciprocate proofreading for each other.

Do not skimp on proofreading. After all the time and effort you put into creating a résumé and cover letter, sourcing a job lead, and responding to it, isn't taking care to ensure flawless application materials really a sensible return on investment?

No Room for Excuses in the Cover Letter

Job Seeker's Story

George was 42, had suffered a mild heart attack, retired early from his high-stress career, and spent two years finishing his bachelor's degree in mechanical engineering. He had his old résumé that focused on his former career, and really did not know how to play up his new engineering skills in the document. George knew he really needed to make the most of his cover letter to get in the door.

In his concise letter he addressed his gaps by talking about the high stress of his last job and the impact on his health leading to his decision to go back to school and pursue a new career. He explained that, although he didn't have any experience, he had a degree, and would work hard and be a dedicated employee. He went on to list all his courses as well as a few skills and what he saw as his strengths in engineering. George felt he had represented his value well despite the fact that his résumé was out of date.

George applied for many positions but did not generate any interviews. He was frustrated that his time and money invested in his education appeared to be a waste.

Job Seeker's Stumble

Addressing negatives of any kind in a cover letter is a mistake. George thought he was doing the right thing by explaining his past problems, but, instead, he was just drawing attention to them. When he applied for a position he might have been one of thousands of applicants, and this would not have helped him to stand out as a well-matched candidate. It would not have marketed his value, but rather focused on his negatives.

Further, George thought that just reserving details of his degree for the letter, and not updating his résumé with them, would be enough. He did not realize that sometimes the letter does not get read, and it is the résumé's job ultimately to present the required details to be a match to the targeted positions.

Job Seeker's ≷New Strategy≷

The best cover letters are written to take into account that applying for a job is a competition among candidates. The letter must grab the busy reviewer's attention with an enticing start followed by a positive focus on relevant experience, strengths, and achievements. Therefore, take the following steps to create a winning letter:

▷ **Seek to Capture Attention in a Positive Manner:** Start the letter with an attention-getter, such as an:

> **Engaging Question:** "Are you seeking a talented and dedicated professional with a solid grounding in Mechanical Engineering?"

> **Interesting Fact or Statistic:** "According to the American Society of Mechanical Engineers there are X million mechanical engineers in the U.S. today. So what makes me different?"

> **Informative Piece About the Company:** "When I read about the pioneering efforts that Alteron Chemicals has made in ____, I knew that my experience in mechanical engineering would allow me to make a positive and sustainable contribution."

> **Applicable Contact or Referral to the Company:** "Thomas Mulhaney, VP of Marketing, suggested that I contact you...."

> **Inspiring Quotation from a Former Boss or Professor:** "George has proven himself to be a highly discerning professional with a keen ability to solve complex mechanical design and fabrication problems. He has been an asset to fellow students and professors, and has been tapped for complex projects that would otherwise be considered above his level...."

▷ **Sell Your Strengths:** Once you have captured the reviewer's attention, it is time to demonstrate your expertise through a strong results-driven paragraph or series of bullets. Never use this section, or any part of the cover letter, to talk about problems or weaknesses. For instance, a career changer would not focus on trying to overcome a lack of experience. He would emphasize what he possessed, such as "*In conjunction with completing my BS in Mechanical Engineering, I had the opportunity to collaborate on a number of projects relevant to your company's needs. For instance, when you review my enclosed résumé you will find that I collaborated with students and staff at Florida Tech on the design and fabrication of a hydrocarbon fuel pretreater apparatus for their Microelectronics Lab.*"

Always remember that your cover letter is a sales tool: Be honest, upbeat, and professional, and emphasize your strengths to show how you are a match for the company and the job.

Hit the Bull's-Eye With a Targeted Cover Letter

Job Seeker's Story

Jasmine was an exceptional consumer-goods and member-ship services Salesperson. She had a real talent for persuasion, relationship-building, and customer service. Her sales track record was stellar, and her enthusiasm was genuine and infectious. When Jasmine decided to move back to her hometown of Richmond (Virginia), she sent out hundreds of cover letters and résumés, including one to a local organization that promoted dating-membership sales. This is the cover letter she wrote in response to every job posting:

> As you will note from the attached résumé, my work experience has been constant, productive, and growth-oriented with progress shown for experience.

> While my work history states positions and responsibilities held, I feel the best area of accomplishment is in skills in communication in dealing with and through people to reach goals and objectives.

> It is my feeling that my attitude and experience will be good in serving both our interests. I look forward to hearing from you in the near future.

Jasmine never did hear back from the dating-membership organization, her top choice, even though she re-sent her cover letter and résumé twice. Her dream sales job in her hometown never materialized, despite her outstanding qualifications.

Job Seeker's Stumble

By trying to cut corners, Jasmine undermined her job search with a generic cover letter, which she used repeatedly, regardless of the position she was pursuing. She assumed that the reviewer would read her résumé and that the cover letter was merely a formality.

Job Seeker's ≥New Strategies≤

Cover letters can play a critical role in the selection process, particularly as a screening-out mechanism. Reviewers want to see targeted responses to their job postings and evidence of interest in and suitability for their posted positions. In Jasmine's case, her cover letter lacked this much-needed specific information. The reader had no idea of what job posting (if any) she was responding to and why she should be considered for employment with their company.

Craft your cover letter by following these three simple steps. Specifically:

▷ **Capture Attention and Establish Interest:** Write the cover letter keeping the self-interest of the reader in mind. Make it clear what position you are applying for and why. Tie your enthusiasm for the position to the employer's needs. For example, Jasmine could have written:

> After reading 'The CONNECT Guide to Dating in Richmond,' I researched your company and discovered, much to my excitement, that you have an opening for a Sales Director. Your description of Sales Directors as 'self-motivated individuals who enjoy making a difference in clients' lives' sounds like it was written just for me. In fact, one of my recent clients described me as 'the most genuine and responsive sales rep I have encountered in 22 years in the business.' This is typical of the kind of client feedback I get.

▷ **Relay Relevant and Convincing Proof:** Take charge of convincing the reader of your top-notch qualifications by citing specific, relevant accomplishments that address every requirement stated. In addition, use quantifiers to demonstrate the scope of your accomplishment for added impact. For example, Jasmine's accomplishments could have been relayed this way:

You will note that my sales qualifications meet all of your requirements as follows:

- **Membership sales.** Ranked number one in membership sales (out of 10-member sales team) for health club memberships in Baltimore, Maryland, for three consecutive years.

- **Proven sales background.** Consistently surpassed average client sales by 30% in current consumer-goods sales position. Won four quarterly team sales awards within two years for imported home furnishings store.

- **Success with Fortune 500 clientele.** Cultivated client relationships with upscale clientele such as physicians, attorneys, CEOs, and business owners that drove repeat and referral sales up to 75% within the first year.

▷ **Stand Out From the Crowd:** After establishing credibility with accomplishments, cement your differentiation from other candidates, who may also demonstrate accomplishments, by conveying the advantages of your personal brand and fit with the company culture.

Jasmine could have said:

Knowing how difficult it can be to bring someone new on board and integrate them into the team, let me assure you that my style of consultative selling and trust-building skills would blend in well with your company's mission of 'providing services that fulfill dreams with confidentiality and integrity.' If you are interested in a candidate that can begin to contribute immediate results like I have done in my previous sales positions, may we meet soon so I can make my case?

Put Professionalism First in Your Cover Letter

Job Seeker's Story

When Tasha, a Recruiter for Horizon Ventures, would advertise for a position, she was always shocked by the poor quality of applications that were received. Tasha had come to expect that she would be throwing away more than half of the submissions due to issues such as glaring typographical errors, unrelated experience, and missing information, but there was one applicant whose cover letter she will never forget.

Tasha was reviewing résumés and cover letters that had been faxed, e-mailed, and mailed to the office, when one caught her eye. Before even looking at the cover letter or résumé, she was stopped in her tracks by a handwritten note that had been stapled to the letter. It seemed that the applicant, who we will call Tina, made a last-second decision to write an addendum to her cover letter. In her haste, she ripped a piece of lined notebook paper out of a spiral notebook and wrote a note indicating that her computer was broken so she could not make changes to the document, but wanted to indicate a change of address and to mention she was applying for the Scientist I position.

Tasha did not find Tina's solution to her computer problems very professional and could not picture her being a detail-oriented employee for any position, let alone that of a scientist. Tasha did not respond to Tina's application, but held out for a candidate who made a professional first impression with her employment documents.

Job Seeker's Stumble

Unfortunately, Tina neglected the golden rule of applying for employment: First impressions are the most important. Because her documents were messy, out-of-date, and unprofessional in appearance, the prospective employer saw her as an individual who would most likely be messy and unprofessional. In short, she was judged by her first presentation, which makes sense when that was all the reviewer had to go on when assessing Tina's candidacy.

Job Seeker's ⇒New Strategy⇐

Your application documents—résumé, cover letter, and anything else you might be submitting—are walking advertisements for you. You can expect to be judged by the way they look and read. Therefore, quality is critical in your cover letter (and other documents). Specifically:

> **Personalize the Letter:** Don't use dated salutations such as *"Dear Sirs,"* as you could be insulting a female reviewer. You should strive to find out who to address. When you cannot identify your target you should use, *"Dear Prospective Employer."*

> **Stay Professional:** Your letter is your calling card, so be professional in content, presentation, paper choice, and submission.

> **Focus on Quality:** Check, double-check, and triple-check your content for errors in spelling, layout, grammar, punctuation, and sentence structure. Additionally, you should opt for dynamic language and a vibrant presentation.

First impressions count, so make the most of yours with a quality presentation in your cover letter.

Selling Yourself out of a Job With Salary History
Job Seeker's Story

After moving from Boston to the small town of Mims (Florida), Marshall was thrilled to find a local opportunity for a Project Administrator at one of the few large companies in the area. He was careful to tailor his résumé and cover letter to match the job requirements, right down to the request to include salary history.

He felt a little twinge of concern about the salary history, as it seemed both pay and cost of living were not as high in this small town compared to what it had been in Boston. However, he knew he should answer the question, so he explained in the final paragraph of his cover letter that his ending salary in his last position had been $80,000.

Marshall was disappointed that he never heard from the company for an interview but assumed it was probably his salary history.

Job Seeker's Stumble

Marshall had the right idea about answering all employer requests and questions, but he did not take advantage of the opportunity to help this prospective employer connect that his salary was based on Boston wages and cost of living, and not that of a small Florida town. In fact, the Boston wage of $80,000 would have been equivalent to around $50,000 in his new location, but, because the reviewer would most likely not look deeply enough into the accompanying résumé, she would just assume that Marshall was way out of the company's budget.

Rarely do employers see it as a positive opportunity to consider a candidate who is outside their budget, because, even if the candidate would accept a reduced salary, the general assumption is that he would be likely to leave as soon as a more lucrative offer were obtained.

Job Seeker's ≥New Strategy≤

Including your salary history can seem to be a lose-lose proposition, as employers use it as a screening tool to cut out applicants who are too high or too low. So why would you include it? Because if you do not, you raise "red flags" with the reviewer for not following directions, appearing difficult, and/ or having something to hide (too high or too low prior salary).

It is actually not that hard to deal with this issue. Just apply the following strategies:

▷   Do not over-think the request if your salary requirements are in the range of the job market. It is not necessary to include an entire starting and ending salary list for your career. Instead, keep it simple with an open response such as *"During the last few years of my career my compensation has been in the $70K range with benefits. I am currently negotiable."*

▷   Help the employer cross the bridge to understand your salary if it is too high or too low for the market. This is particularly important if you have made too much based on a different cost of living or are changing fields. For example, you might say, *"Having just relocated from Boston, I recognize that my $80,000 salary is equivalent to a salary in the $50–60K range in this market. I believe compensation should reflect both professional ability and market trends, and am therefore currently negotiable in my requirements."*

▷   Keep your salary history details clear, concise, and positive within the cover letter. Additionally, it is a good idea to always include that you are *"currently negotiable,"* as it can make an employer more willing to speak with you. It does not mean you are opening yourself up to low offers, but that you want to see if there is a fit for your skills and a fitting salary for that contribution.

CHAPTER 4

Follow-Up Letter Follies

∧

Creativity Goes Over the Top and out the Door

Job Seeker's Story

Jorge was interviewing for an Account Executive position at a marketing firm where the competition was fierce. He left the first interview feeling very positive and decided that he would win the job by standing out with a memorable follow-up strategy. Jorge went to a local discount retail store and bought a pair of black business shoes in a whopping size 13. He left one shoe in the box and had it couriered to the interviewer with a note that said, *"I'd do anything to get my foot in the door."*

Time passed and Jorge did not receive a return call or a second interview, which surprised him. When he followed up he was told that someone else was selected. He could not help but ask what the interviewer thought of the shoe. The interviewer responded, *"We expect something new and creative at a marketing company of our caliber. Frankly, we've seen the shoe gimmick before, and were unimpressed and rather disappointed with the shoddy display of marketing strategy you obviously possess."*

Job Seeker's Stumble

Jorge targeted a cutting-edge marketing firm with a dated strategy that made his presentation come across as stale and gimmicky. Without it, he might have literally been a "shoe-in" for the job. Although there is truly a place for out-of-the-box approaches to follow up, it is critical to ensure you are choosing one that is not dated, overused, or inappropriate for the position or company you have targeted.

Job Seeker's ≷New Strategies≷

In most situations, a professional follow-up letter that allows you to sell your strengths and make up for any perceived weaknesses from the interview is most appropriate. However, there are strategies you can use to make a positive impression beyond the letter:

▷ Include a few reference letters that demonstrate your strengths for the position.

▷ Write a white paper or report that further demonstrates your expertise in the area of your targeted position or that shows how you would handle a challenge the company is facing.

▷ Provide a sample of your work and/or a link to a Web portfolio on the Internet.

Though a creative follow-up may seem to be a great idea to stand out from the crowd, it is important to make sure you are making the right choice. Be sure to:

▷ **Know Your Target:** If you do not have a sense of the employer's personality and how he will appreciate a creative follow-up, then it is best to avoid one.

▷ **Gauge Appropriateness:** Do not be creative for creativity's sake. If you are not in a creative industry, then a creative follow-up is probably not your best bet.

▹ **Apply a Fresh Approach:** When you opt for creativity, strive to be flawless, innovative, and unique in your effort. Do not think that using colored paper or a colored font is enough. Additionally, gag-like gimmicks are not appropriate for professional positions.

Consider a few examples of how creativity has been used effectively by job seekers:

> A Sales Executive and Advertising Professional for the surf-wear industry used her desktop publishing software to create a full-color custom label to wrap around a bar of surf wax manufactured by the company. She sent the bar to the interviewer with a follow-up letter talking about "customizing service to each client."

> A Mural Artist created a custom work of art, scanned it into the computer, mapped it out as a puzzle, superimposed a creative version of her résumé that placed one topic area per puzzle section, printed it in full-color, mounted it on foam backing, and cut out the pieces. Along with the puzzle she included an uncut puzzle and a letter stressing that she could put all the pieces together in this role.

> A Web Designer demonstrated his grasp of design techniques the company was not using by creating a mock-up of a new service Web page and including the URL to the page in his follow-up letter.

> An Interior Designer created a 3D mock-up of a room design for her prospective client.

> A Dietician brought a booklet of sample nutrition plans she had created for previous clients.

When in doubt, go for a follow-up strategy that is productive and effective instead of creative just for creativity's sake, because more often than not, creativity will do more harm than good.

Do Not Shoot Yourself in the Foot

Job Seeker's Story

Mark, a medical-products Sales Manager, was sure he had aced his interview with a medical-equipment distributor. After all, he and the Vice President of Sales really hit it off; so much so, they had a three-and-a-half-hour interview! Mark knew the importance of following up after the interview and immediately sent the VP a faxed thank-you letter.

When Mark did not hear from the VP after one week, he followed up again with a phone call and left a message expressing his interest in the position and inquiring about when the hiring decision would be made. With no response from the VP, Mark continued to leave phone and e-mail messages, and even followed up with mailed copies of his original faxed thank-you letter.

After four weeks of no communication from the interviewer, Mark decided he had to bring the process to conclusion. He penned the following letter to the VP of Sales:

> For the past four weeks I have tried repeatedly using various methods to contact you and get an update on our interview outcome. I can only assume since you spent 3 ½ hours with me that you have an interest in my qualifications. Since you will not respond, I want to encourage you by sending along with this letter a $5.00 bill. This should motivate you to respond to me. Everybody is motivated by money.

Mark felt this last-attempt letter would surely result in a positive response—a job offer. To his surprise, Mark never heard from the interviewer concerning his job status, and never saw his $5 bill again.

Job Seeker's Stumble

Although Mark was meeting his need to bring conclusion to the interview process, he did so in a way that was confrontational and derogatory. Beware of offending the interviewer by making assumptions about the interviewer's motives for not responding, or by attempting a "bribe" to expedite the decision-making process.

Job Seeker's ≥New Strategies≤

Waiting to hear back from the hiring authority after an interview can be an excruciating experience, primarily because the locus of control is out of your hands. Do what you can to positively influence the hiring decision by staying in touch via alternating one-way (letters, e-mails, and faxes) and two-way (phone calls) communications. Do not bribe, cajole, reprimand, or instruct the interviewer in what you believe should be appropriate action.

In your follow-up letters you may want to include well-researched company and industry information to further illustrate your intense interest in the company and to point out additional examples of skills and accomplishments that make you a top-notch candidate. Your phone messages can be brief and businesslike, requesting feedback on your status and offering to provide additional proof of suitability and references.

After four to six weeks with no feedback whatsoever from the interviewer, the likelihood exists that you are no longer in the running. Do not rely on one interview, no matter how promising, to deter you from continuing in your job search. If you pursue other job leads and go on interviews, even while you are awaiting a final decision, you will feel more in control of your job search fate. Most of all, you will be less likely to shoot yourself in the foot with a last-ditch, desperate attempt at closure.

Missing the Marketing Mark Without Personalization
Job Seeker's Story

George arrived on time and appropriately dressed in a suit and tie for his logistics management interview with

Ms. Meeley, Director of Human Resources. He was familiar with the company and prepared to ask questions that showed his interest in the firm. In short, he did a great job of making a positive impression.

Unfortunately, as George was leaving the office, he turned to Ms. Meeley, shook her hand, thanked her for her time, and handed her a sealed envelope. Surprised, she asked, *"What is this?"*

George responded proudly, *"That's my thank-you letter. I even included a self-addressed stamped envelope so you can easily follow up with me about the position."*

Ms. Meeley was surprised but recovered quickly, thanking George for his time and walking him to the door. Later, when she reviewed the letter she discovered a short, generic, handwritten note that said:

Dear hiring authority,

I appreciate your taking the time to meet with me today to discuss your position. Your insight into the position and the organization's needs was most helpful. I am confident that I will be able to be a strong asset for your company.

Please do not hesitate to call me or use the enclosed SASE to send any correspondence.

Sincerely,

George C. Joseph

Job Seeker's Stumble

Some might feel that George was acting proactively by being ready with a thank-you letter at the end of the interview. However, this type of action would, more often than not, leave a poor impression. Why? Though it might seem proactive, it was actually perceived as lazy; anyone could write up the generic letter that George wrote without bothering to take the time to learn the name of the interviewer or connect specific events in the interview within the letter.

Further, this strategy stripped George of the opportunity to create a thoughtful response that allowed him to play up his strengths for the position and to enhance his positive interview presentation.

Job Seeker's ≥New Strategies≤

George did one thing right: He knew he needed a letter. Unfortunately, the vast majority of interviewees never write a letter. A thank-you letter is more than a pleasant courtesy and an opportunity for a job seeker to sell himself for the job. In many cases, the employer expects it, and will eliminate a candidate who does not write one.

▷ **Understand Why You Need a Thank-You Letter:** A thank-you letter:

> Shows courtesy toward the interviewer for his or her time.

> Conveys your interest in the position.

> Provides you an opportunity to get back in front of the employer again, in case you have faded into the memory of an employer who has met too many people.

> Allows you to introduce information you neglected in the interview or didn't do a great job introducing.

▷ **Avoid Common Mistakes:** Don't:

> Send generic or canned thank-you letters.

> Fax or e-mail thank-you letters. (Of course, if all communication has been by e-mail and the employer will be traveling, the rules change.)

> Hand a thank-you letter to the employer at the end of the interview.

> Forget to sign the letter.

▷ **Include Common Letter Elements:** Your letter should:

> Highlight what the employer liked about you.

> Cover positive information you wish you had said in the interview.

> Express your skill in areas in which the employer showed concer.

> Make a positive impact.

> Ask for the next step in the interview process.

▷ **Apply Easy Steps to Capture the Essence of the Interview for Your Letter:** Each time you leave an interview, you can be assured you will be ready to make the most of your thank-you letter if you:

> Make sure to have the full name, correct spelling, and title of each interviewer before you leave. Asking for business cards is a great way to do this. NOTE: It is a very good idea to send an individual letter to each person with whom you met.

> Directly following the interview, jot down answers to the following:

  ✓ Key questions that were asked.

  ✓ Answers that captured their interest or which they said represented important skills for the position's requirements or organization's challenges.

  ✓ Concerns they voiced.

  ✓ Information you wish you had shared in regard to their requests.

  By jotting that information down, you will be prepared to return home and flesh out a personalized letter to the interviewer(s) that expresses your interest, reiterates your strengths and match for the position, and overcomes any interviewer concerns.

▷ **Write Your Letter:** Now you have all the ingredients to gather the right information and write the best thank-you letter.

The Simple Things Can Hurt the Most

Job Seeker's Story

Beth wanted to provide a personal yet professional approach to her interview follow-up. So she purchased a thank-you card and wrote a short note thanking the interviewer for her time, letting her know that she looked forward to the next step, and expressing her continued interest in becoming a part of the team. She sent it out the afternoon of her interview and received a call a few days later to meet with the interviewer in a group interview.

During the interview she was told that the company had used handwriting analysis on her letter and had concerns about her match. She was taken completely off guard, and, although she silently did not agree with their findings, she professionally defended herself against their concerns and provided positive responses. Despite her efforts, she did not get the job.

Job Seeker's Stumble

Handwriting analysis may come as a surprise, but it is more common than you think. In fact, a 2007 survey of Human Resources professionals by the professional association Career Directors International found that 2 percent of companies have used handwriting analysis and 16 percent said they would consider using it.

Handwriting any documentation for a prospective employer could subject you to handwriting analysis, and it could also leave you open to misinterpretation. For instance, if your handwriting is hard to read it could leave a negative impression, just as much as dotting your letter "i" with a heart could.

Job Seeker's ≳New Strategies≲

The company you are targeting may not use handwriting analysis, but the bigger picture is to be aware of how your actions could help or harm in every stage of your job search, interviewing, and negotiation process. In the case of the follow-up letter, not only are there risks of showing a lack of professionalism with a handwritten note, but there is also the issue that you will lose out on a critical opportunity to sell yourself by crafting a strategic follow-up letter.

A note lets you say *"thank you," "consider me,"* and *"I look forward to the next step."* A professional letter, created on the computer, will let you have the space to:

> Thank the interviewer for his or her time.

> Reiterate your strengths for the position.

> Overcome any perceived weaknesses in the interview with a positive spin.

> Share information that was forgotten/neglected during the interview.

> Inquire about the next step and express interest in the position.

In short, a follow-up letter provides you with a powerful second chance to get back in front of the employer and sell yourself for the job. Do not take this opportunity lightly, because it can be a leveraging point that can make or break your introduction to a second interview.

To Follow Up or Not to Follow Up

Job Seeker's Story

Bob, an experienced Computer Engineer, secured an interview with a highly sought-after company based on his great credentials listed in his résumé. However, in the interview, he was shy and nervous, and just could not seem to express himself well. The interview ended poorly and Bob left discouraged.

Bob discussed his lackluster interview performance with a professional résumé writer who recommended a thank-you letter to try to save the situation. Bob questioned whether that would really have any impact. Further, he was so embarrassed about the interview, he wondered what he could even say to recapture the employer's interest. Together, Bob and the résumé writer crafted a two-page letter that contained many salient points that Bob wished he had made in the interview. Because he had not brought letters of recommendation to the interview, they decided to enclose one that glowingly described his skills and accomplishments.

Early the next week, Bob was asked in for a second interview. He was relieved to have gotten that far in the interview process, and was much more at ease. Everything went smoothly and he ultimately ended up being offered, and accepting, the job. Bob found out much later that his employer initially thought he must have falsified his résumé and application because he had performed so poorly in the interview. However, after receiving Bob's thank-you letter, the employer did reference checking and gave him another chance in a second interview, where he proved himself.

Imagine if Bob had not followed up! He certainly would not have landed his job with this employer, and the hit to his self-esteem would likely have damaged his future interview efforts.

Job Seeker's Stumble
Many job seekers miss out on a golden opportunity for further self-marketing by not sending a follow-up letter. According to a 2008 survey by Accountemps of 1,000 executives polled from multiple disciplines (including human resources, marketing, and finance), 88 percent of executives asserted that sending a thank-you letter after an interview can boost a candidate's chances. But, whether due to excessive self-confidence, time constraints, or even embarrassment (as in Bob's case), the majority of job seekers do not follow up after an interview with a thank-you letter. Even fewer candidates use the follow-up letter effectively as a vehicle to entice the employer to move on to the next step: the job offer!

Job Seeker's ≳New Strategies≲

If you think of the interview process in stages, the post-interview phase can be even more critical in generating a job offer than the actual interview. Why would you spend time researching the company and position, practicing interview responses to probable questions, and navigating a highly stressful situation such as an interview, and then let the final outcome be determined by the employer's ever-fading memory of you? That would be similar to preparing months for a 10K marathon race, and then dropping out before the final mile.

Refresh the employer's memory of your exceptional candidacy by creating and sending (within 24 hours) a thank-you letter that reinforces your top-of-mind status, overcomes potential objections, and makes it easy for the employer to see a high return on investment (ROI) for hiring you. According to the survey mentioned previously, 52 percent of executives polled preferred to receive a hand-written thank-you; 44 percent preferred an e-mail follow-up after the interview. Why not do both? Send the email thank-you first, followed by a well-thought-out thank-you letter that briefly and clearly overcomes any objections that might have been raised in the interview and reminds the interviewer of your points of differentiation and value.

Send a separate and customized thank-you letter to every person who interviewed you; they may compare notes! Continue to follow up periodically to check on the status of your candidacy. Find opportunities to build increasing evidence that you are really the only candidate worth serious consideration, and bring that to the interviewer(s) attention. Send follow-up articles and/or tidbits of information you have found that demonstrate your knowledge of the industry and latest trends, as well as your willingness to share that information with others on your team.

CHAPTER 5

Job Search Jinxes

∧

Don't Wait for the Phone to Ring

Job Seeker's Story

Bob invested in a professional résumé that would best show-case his experience. As soon as it was completed, he began applying to engineering positions on Internet job boards.

After applying for more than 50 positions, Bob had received little response beyond auto responses telling him that the résumé had been received.

When he contacted his writer, Bonnie, he was very upset. He let her know the new document was not working. She took the time to question him on how he was using the résumé in his job search. Once he had told her that he was applying to adver-tised positions on major job boards, she was able to pinpoint the likely cause of the problem: his limited job search.

Bonnie explained that he was applying for highly visible positions that received a tremendous number of responses, which could number in the hundreds and even thousands. She shared that Human Resources departments were overworked and did not have the staff to view all the submissions they were receiving. Further, she told him that some résumés would never arrive due to SPAM traps and other e-mail issues. She told Bob that, although he had an excellent résumé, it was of little use unless he could improve his chances of getting it viewed by putting it in front of real hiring personnel and decision-makers, as well as following up to ensure it reached its destination.

Job Seeker's Stumble

As so commonly happens with this number-one job search mistake, Bob was lured by the many job opportunities on the Internet into believing he just needed to apply and he would receive interviews. With the number of positions that are posted, it would seem that this should be an easy and effective job search method. This can sometimes be the case, but it is similar to a game of chance, where the odds are rarely in your favor. This is due to the number of applicants applying for the position, as well as other barriers that can occur (such as employers freezing opportunities or not actually being in active hiring mode, but rather seeking to test the market).

Job Seeker's ≷New Strategy≷

When using the Internet in your job search, you need to use it as only one part of your job search. Some of the best ways are to:

▷ **See Who Is Hiring:** By viewing job postings you can identify employers that are actively hiring. Once you know who they are, you can visit their Websites to identify other opportunities and learn more about them.

▷ **Find Recruiters and Temporary Agencies:** Recruiters and agencies post opportunities, so viewing ads on the Internet can also be a good way to identify other opportunities.

▷ **Determine Salary Ranges:** Some posted positions will include salary information, which can give you a good idea of salary ranges. Additional sites for salary information include *www.salary.com* and *www.payscale.com.*

Once you have found an opportunity on the Internet that interests you, it is a good idea to determine how much effort to exert in the application process based on how close a match you are to the job opportunity. You might use a ranking scale. For example:

> A = job is a perfect match/very close match to job target and experience
>
> B = job is pretty close but I am missing some minor/major requirements
>
> C = job looks as if it could be interesting but I am not a good match
>
> D = job has some elements that I am uncertain about but I would still like to check it out

For an A-ranked opportunity, you would go above and beyond the instructions for application provided in the job listing. After you follow their directions, you should apply two strategies:

1. Follow up with Human Resources to attempt to make a contact and ensure your résumé was received.

2. Research to identify the actual person who this position would report to so that you can mail him your résumé and cover letter.

Sometimes it is easy to put a phone call through to Human Resources and reach a live person, but other times it is impossible. In cases where you can reach someone, you should say, *"My name is _____, and I recently applied for your Engineering position posted on your Website. I can imagine you are bombarded by résumés and I realize e-mail is not always an exact science, so I was just calling to see if I could verify that my résumé was received."*

Be cordial and professional. If you reach someone who seems helpful, you might also add, *"I truly feel I have a lot to offer <Company Name> and wonder if you could share any of your expertise with me on how I can improve my chances of being considered for this opportunity?"*

Powerful forces are at work when you treat someone as an expert and ask for advice. You may find yourself the recipient of some very helpful advice that you can put to use, or, at the least, a contact you can thank and follow up with in the future.

The worst scenario for contacting Human Resources is that you reach an individual who is not interested in speaking with you. If it is a large company, you might consider trying to call at different times of the day in an attempt to reach another member of the department. Otherwise, remember that the squeaky wheel gets the grease; just stay professional and courteous!

To find the actual "boss-to-be" you may have to do a little more work. This could be as easy as visiting the company's Website and doing some research, or talking to your local or social networking contacts. When you cannot find a name, you need to call the company directly. However, if you say you are a job seeker, you will always end up transferred to Human Resources or referred to the company's Website. Instead, it is time to put on that detective hat and ferret out the information. For instance, consider this scenario:

Bob needed to find the Vice President of Engineering, so he called the company and reached the phone system. He selected to be connected to accounting and, when the phone was answered, he said in a fast and somewhat harried sounding voice, *"I'm so sorry to bother you. I thought I was calling the engineering department, but maybe you can help me and save me the embarrassment. My name is Tom Miller, and I was supposed to send over some paperwork that my boss had discussed with your Director of Engineering yesterday. But, oh I can't believe this, I've misplaced his information and my boss is going to kill me. I'm trying to find it out without having to tell him what I have done. Can you help me? I just need his name."*

If making up a name and using someone else's phone makes you feel uncomfortable, then your best bet is to get a trusted friend or family member to make the call, because they have nothing to lose in the process, and any errors they make will not lead back to you.

Alternatively, another route is to call acting as a student. For instance, *"I am currently completing a business management course through the XYZ University. For this class I need to research and make a list of top Engineering VPs in my local market. After reading about your company on your Website, I would like to include your VP's name. Could you provide that for me?"*

Once you have uncovered this information, personalize your cover letter, print it and your résumé on high-quality paper, and place them in a 9 x 12 white catalog envelope. You should neatly print the address and mark the envelope *confidential* in the bottom left corner, because personalized mail and confidential mail tends to be opened more often than labeled mail.

You have taken all these steps for the "A" ranked position, and why? This is where your résumé would most likely end up if it had not been lost or discarded in Human Resources. You leapfrog over all the competition by putting your résumé directly in front of the decision-maker.

Now, if your opportunity is ranked as a "B," you will most likely take the same steps as for the "A" positions. However, you will have to determine how much time you have and how interested you are in the opportunity to determine how far you are willing to go in this time-consuming process.

For "C" and "D" opportunities, you will probably opt to follow the application instructions only, because these positions represent the lowest possibility of a match and therefore are not the best use of your time in job searching.

Be sure to augment your Internet job search with techniques involving networking, which is considered to be the best way to find a job. There are numerous ways to network locally with friends, colleagues, and former coworkers and bosses, and on the Internet through social networking sites such as *www.linkedin.com* and *www.facebook.com.*

By expanding your approach to applying for job opportunities beyond the Internet, you will increase the speed with which you will find your next job.

Job Search Scams Abound—Be Wary!

Job Seeker's Story

Clara had been engaged in her job search for quite some time, but had not seen the results she anticipated. A customer service/account manager in her early 30s, Clara had a professionally prepared résumé that delighted her, and she felt it represented her well. In fact, it had won her several interviews, but alas, no job offers—yet. She had resisted working more closely with a career coach, because she was very concerned about spending the money when she felt she might be laid off at any moment due to her employer's announced right-sizing program.

On a cold February evening, she once again felt compelled to peruse the local newspaper's classified ad section. Her heart leapt when a new display ad captured her attention. The ad for "National Account Managers" and "Customer Service Professionals" was placed by a company headquartered in Florida. There was a toll-free telephone number listed to call for more information, and she circled it with her yellow highlighter. *"What possible harm could there be in a little anonymous telephone call?"* she thought.

Clara was favorably impressed when her phone call was answered on the first ring by a friendly sounding woman who responded to all of Clara's questions. It turned out this company had placed ads throughout the Northeast, aware that folks might be especially interested in considering relocation during the harsh western New York winters. *"How terribly clever of them!"* Clara thought, increasingly impressed.

The highly professional company representative, Sondra, asked several probing questions about Clara's background and qualifications, and, based upon her responses, expressed strong interest in forwarding her name to the "candidate pool."

Sondra was very complimentary toward Clara, who indulged in a bit of pride that she had actually spent some time in preparing for a telephone interview just last weekend, and felt she had conducted herself quite well. She was positively thrilled to receive a phone call the next day, inviting her to interview at their corporate headquarters in Boca Raton. She had made the cut! Excitement coursed through her veins, as she struggled to focus on Sondra's instructions.

Sondra asked if she could be available to travel just five days hence. Yes, Clara could make that work. *"They must be really interested in me,"* thought Clara. Sondra then explained that, to streamline the logistics, it would be far better for Clara's travel arrangements to be coordinated from there, as they could command corporate air and hotel rates far more economically than Clara could on her own. *"Great! That makes perfect sense,"* thought Clara.

When Sondra asked Clara to wire transfer $450, Clara hesitated. Sondra quickly explained that it would simply save time for Clara as she wouldn't have to bother with all that pesky paperwork in submitting her travel expenses after the interview. When Clara still seemed a bit reluctant, Sondra confided that the company had been "stiffed" by a couple of job candidates who had seemed sincere enough, but who, when Sondra had mailed them their airline tickets, had absconded. Not only did this damage the company (no interviewees and loss of money), but Sondra further confided that it had been a profound professional embarrassment to her. Sondra explained that wiring the money was "merely a show of good faith" on Clara's part, and she would be reimbursed in full at the time of the interview in only five days' time.

After speaking with Sondra, who sounded so professional, enthusiastic, and warm, Clara concluded that, because her local job search had stalled, a few sunny days in Florida would lift her spirits and perhaps lead to new employment. She wired the money that same day.

When Clara called to confirm receipt of her fund transfer and to finalize the details of her trip with Sondra, she was astonished to discover that the telephone number was no longer in service. Contacting directory assistance revealed that there was no listing for the corporation anywhere in Florida— nor, in fact, anywhere in the continental United States.

Job Seeker's Stumble

Clara was taken in by a scam operation and only discovered her mistake when it was too late. Her lack of due diligence in researching the prospective company and its potential job openings, combined with her trusting nature, left her open to a common form of fraud that relies on desperate job seekers.

Job Seeker's ≳New Strategy≲

Reputable employers, whether in the private, non-profit, or governmental sector, generally do not require job candidates to forward money for any reason, under any circumstances. They may ask a candidate to pay travel expenses out of pocket and then submit those expenses for reimbursement. Depending on the circumstances, an employer may also tell the candidate that there will be no reimbursement for travel to the interview, in which case the candidate can decide whether it's worth spending the money to make the trip. Either way, Clara might have been far better off to have made her own travel arrangements. If Sondra had resisted this, then red flags and alarm bells should have squelched any thoughts of pursuing this so-called opportunity, no matter how sunny the prospects may have seemed.

Although it is perfectly acceptable to respond to classified ads in a job search, it is highly recommended to do so only after one has conducted research on the company in question, particularly when the ad includes the name of the company! Frequently, such research (especially online) will turn up news articles, for example, that may reveal information about any ongoing investigations or irregularities previously encountered by the potential employer. Chambers of commerce, the Better Business Bureau, the U.S. Attorney General's Office, the Federal Citizen's Information Center (FCIC) for Scams and Frauds, and the Privacy Rights Clearinghouse's article on "Avoiding Online Job Scams" are all online resources for fraud alerts and detection. Doing financial research via online search capabilities, such as Edgar Online, can also yield critically important information in the due diligence process.

In addition to online research and a quick visit to the local public library, it's always a good idea to activate one's professional networking contacts online and offline. The "six degrees of separation" theory typically holds up quite well, and usually someone in the network will turn up information about the target employer. This "insider" information frequently proves invaluable, and may make all the difference in a job search.

Sadly, con artists exist even in the job search arena, and motivated candidates need to be mindful that no matter how desperate one's circumstances may seem to be, ultimately the old adage "buyer beware!" remains only too valid.

The importance of seriously evaluating one's investment (financial, intellectual, emotional, and more) in one's career is worth discussing. How much is it worth to take every possible action to ensure that one's next job is a good fit? In the process of investigating the business background and financial standing of the company mentioned in the ad to uncover its products and services, and to determine if she was genuinely interested in the company, Clara probably would have discovered the scam and steered clear. Instead, Clara was enticed by the perceived opportunity and felt that $450 was a "reasonable investment." How much different might the outcome have been for Clara had she instead invested her time and energies into preliminary research? At the very least, she would still have had her $450 to actually take a Florida vacation!

Multiple Résumés Can Lead to Employer Confusion

Job Seeker's Story

Sam's career in Information Technology (IT) started off slowly after college graduation with a Help Desk job for a consumer-products company. When Sam did not get a promotion after one year with the company, he decided he needed to acquire the best position possible with the best rate and advancement opportunities available. Because he had heard that networking was a good job-search method, he prepared and sent a résumé to a friend who was employed at a mid-sized company that Sam had targeted for his job search efforts. Sam asked his friend to be on the lookout for a suitable opening for which he could apply. As an afterthought, Sam added that his friend could "pass along" his résumé to whomever his friend felt would be able to help Sam secure an IT job at the company.

The résumé Sam wrote for his friend indicated he was open for any IT job, although he only had experience in Help Desk support. On the résumé Sam detailed his requirements for the job he was seeking—a bulleted list of salary and benefits "must-haves"—in the Objective statement, which took up the top half of the one-page résumé. The bottom half of the résumé briefly covered his work history and education. In his cover letter to his friend, Sam included sarcastic jabs at his current supervisor and company. Sam really piled it on about how his current company did not recognize his skills, how his boss was incompetent and Sam could really do his job, and how the company was still in the "dinosaur age" when it came to computers and information technology.

After sending the résumé and letter to his friend, Sam decided that, because he had made the effort to write a résumé, he might as well revise it a bit to make it more "professional," and send it to the CEO of the company where his friend was employed. He took out the requirements bulleted in the Objective, and augmented his work history with excerpts from his current job description, a listing of college courses he had taken, and his technology skills. With this revamped résumé, Sam included a one-paragraph cover letter asking for an IT job, and mailed it directly to the CEO, whose name he had gotten from his friend.

To Sam's utter delight and amazement, he was contacted by the CEO's secretary, who promptly scheduled a morning interview for Sam with the CEO. Sam reasoned that his résumé had been so compelling and that his talents were so obvious, the CEO himself had decided to conduct the interview. Sam felt so sure a job offer was coming from the CEO that he took off the day from his Help Desk job to celebrate right after the interview and forthcoming job offer.

When Sam was escorted into the CEO's office, the CEO shook his hand and then indicated a high-backed chair across the desk from him where Sam was to sit.

After Sam settled in, the CEO held up the résumé and cover letter Sam had sent to him and asked, *"Are these the application materials that you sent to me?"*

Sam quickly replied, *"Yes—and thank you for reading it and inviting me in to interview."*

The CEO smiled briefly and then held up a second set of materials: the résumé and much-longer letter Sam had sent to his friend who was employed at this company. *"Is this also your résumé and cover letter?"*

Sam could not understand how this version of his résumé and cover letter had gotten into the hands of the CEO. After all, he had sent this version to his friend. Then he remembered he had asked his friend to "pass along" the résumé for him. Apparently his friend had conveyed the résumé and longer (more sarcastic) cover letter to the Human Resources department who, in turn, passed it "up the line" to the CEO's office! All Sam could do was meekly answer, *"Yes."*

At that point, the CEO questioned Sam further, *"I'm confused. Which of these two sets of documents do you think I should believe? The one where you make demands for employment and ridicule your current boss and company, or the polite, more professional version?"*

Turning red, Sam had no satisfactory response. The interview ended quickly, without a job offer, and Sam returned home to ponder how he could have better handled the situation.

Job Seeker's Stumble

Sam made three errors in judgment in this scenario:

1. Crafting a demanding and sarcastic set of application materials (résumé and cover letter), which he sent to someone at the company where he wanted to be hired.

2. Asking someone within that company to pass along that set of materials to further his job search efforts.

3. Re-applying to the same company with a vastly different kind of résumé and cover letter, expecting that the two sets of materials would never be compared.

Job Seeker's ≳New Strategy≲

Although Sam did not intend that his two sets of application materials would be compared by the CEO of the company where he was eager to be hired, it was most certainly inevitable. Submissions of application materials, including résumés, are often carefully tracked by HR departments due to federal and internal job-applicant submission policies and procedures. Thus, when Sam's friend conveyed Sam's résumé to HR as an "employee referral," Sam's original, demanding résumé and cover letter were "in play," just as much as the more professional résumé and cover letter he sent directly to the CEO.

There are two learning points in this story: be aware of how important employee referrals are in companies' searches for talent, and be consistent with your résumé "story" and target across all the approach methods you make to a particular company. Let's examine each learning point:

1. **Employee referrals are powerful.** According to a 2007 survey by CareerXRoads for Zoominfo.com called "CareerXRoads Annual Sources of Hire Survey," employee referrals constitute the vast majority (95 percent) of referrals for external-source candidates (not internal promotions or transfers). This can definitely work in your favor as you expand your networking online and offline. In fact, many companies offer hiring bonuses to employees whose referrals result in successful candidates being hired. Just be sure not to give your networking referral a generic résumé; rather, determine your target job (functional area) within the organization and use that target consistently in every application to the company.

2. **Multiple, dissimilar résumés confound the application process.** Whether scanned into a company's internal Applicant Tracking Systems (ATS) due to an employee referral or submitted via online applications, all résumés entered into the applicant database reside there for anywhere from six months to a few years. (Company policies vary on this depending on their resources and needs.)

Consequently, all résumés submitted to a particular company with your name could, in fact, be readily compared.

You may decide to submit more than one résumé to a company because there is more than one job posting you are qualified for and interested in, and that's fine. Quite often similar job postings with different job titles and reference numbers can occur within the same functional area in a company. You will want to custom-tailor your résumé and cover letter in response to each one of those job postings.

However, if those job openings are in vastly different functional areas (say, IT and Human Resources Management), the hiring authorities will be confused when they see résumés submitted by you with different job targets. They may question your interest in and commitment to either occupational field and, hence, your commitment to staying with their company should you be hired. So think carefully before sending multiple résumés to the same company. How would you fare should they be compared? Do you appear to be the same person on both résumés, with the same career goals and motives? Or do you appear to be on a "fishing expedition" for any kind of job, no matter what the functional area or job title? Maximize your candidacy and eliminate employment-reviewer confusion with career-target consistency and personal credibility across multiple résumés.

Is Your Job Target Realistic?

Job Seeker's Story

Cheryl had kept busy with church volunteerism and job search activities after she was laid off from her accounting position. One of her church projects involved heading up the committee that solicited donations from church members for an international organization that supplied stoves to women in foreign countries. When Cheryl saw an online job posting for a position as International Coalition Coordinator, organizing

and leading international-coalition projects across several con-
tinents, she felt compelled to apply based on her church-
project experience. Though she did not meet the specific
requirements, she felt she certainly could learn to handle the
job based on how quickly she had learned to manage the church
fund-raising project for an international organization.

Eleanor, a retired school administrator, needed a part-
time job to augment her retirement income so she could do
more traveling with her husband and their children's families.
As Eleanor scoured the many online Websites for part-time
employment, she came across a job posting for a Hospitality
Teacher at a local resort center only 5miles from her home.
"How perfect!" Eleanor thought as she hurriedly applied with
her old school-administrator résumé and a cover letter. The
cover letter outlined the 35 years of family vacations she had
planned and organized, which had included all aspects of hospitality planning: air transportation, hotel lodging, tours and
entertainment, and meals. *"Surely,"* Eleanor reasoned, *"having done that for 35 years qualifies me to be a Hospitality Teacher!"*
Despite the job posting's requirement of five years of experience in hospitality management, Eleanor decided that, because
this was a part-time job, the resort center would be "flexible"
about that requirement.

Barbra, with a background as a waitress and childcare provider, had recently acquired a bachelor's degree in sociology.
As she searched for job opportunities in the want ads, she came
across one entitled Marketing Director, Assisted Living. When
Barbra consulted a professional résumé writer to compose her
résumé and cover letter for this position, she was asked why
she felt she was qualified for the position, because the ad speci-
fied five years of experience in marketing. Barbra's reply was
simple: *"For 10 years I took my grandmother and aging aunt to
the market every week to do their shopping. That should definitely
qualify me!"*

Job Seeker's Stumble

In these case studies, each job seeker made one or more unrealistic assumptions that were not accurate, and based in wishful thinking. These included assuming that:

> Specific requirements in a job posting are really not "mandatory" requirements.

> Being eager and willing to learn makes up for any lack of requirements.

> Part-time employment does not demand the same rigorous standards of qualifications as full-time employment.

> Having a vague understanding of what a job's duties and responsibilities is all that's needed to determine if there is a match between job and applicant.

> Applying to any job that even remotely matches with my background is a good idea.

Job Seeker's ≥New Strategy≤

Employment reviewers receive high volumes of résumés from applicants comparable to the ones in the earlier case studies, all unqualified for the position listed but nonetheless making the effort to apply. These applicants get screened out quickly from the candidate pool. If you want to avoid wasting time, money, and energy on unrealistic job-search targets, review the following list of questions for every job opening you are considering.

1. **Do you meet all of the specific requirements as listed for the job opening?** Requirements listed on job announcements carry weight precisely because they are easy "screening-out" mechanisms to whittle down the number of applicants to a reasonable pool of candidates. Understand that these are very real hurdles. As you read a specific job posting,

bear in mind that the higher the requirement on the list the more likely it is non-negotiable. So, if a bachelor's degree in communications or marketing is listed first for a Marketing Director position, and the ability to multitask is listed last, the first requirement is going to be a "must-have," and the last one a "would be nice to have" requirement. Typically, educational, licensure, certification, and work experience requirements are the least negotiable items in a job requirements listing, unless the job posting specifies that "substitutions" are acceptable. Applying to job openings for which you do not meet the minimum requirements is a long shot. Even if you know an "insider" who can negotiate an interview for you with the hiring authority, how will that person be able to "make your case" to his superior if you are lacking the significant requirements for the job?

2. **Do you fully understand the job's duties and responsibilities?** Sometimes it is easy to misunderstand what a job is all about, especially if you have never done it before. In Barbra's case study we can see that her understanding of the word *marketing* did not conform to the definition of the word in "Marketing Director." Read the job posting carefully, not only to understand the qualifications and requirements, but also to understand what the job actually entails. If the want ad or job posting does not spell out the job duties and responsibilities, you can research the term (put it in quotation marks in a Google search) to find links to other job postings or articles. You can also research job titles and job descriptions at the Department of Labor's O'Net Center.

3. **Does this job, in this industry, seem interesting enough to you that you could do it well and with commitment?** After gathering and reading more in-depth information about the job description, try to picture yourself doing the actual job.

Would your day seem boring or fulfilling? Would you feel confident and comfortable, or ill at ease because you don't know the terminology or the tasks? If you are undecided, you may want to inquire within your online and offline network for more realistic renditions of what it's like to do that particular kind of job.

In addition, find out about the industry and occupational outlook, and possible career pathways from your network, as well as online resources such as the Career Guide to Industries, Vault, and the Occupational Outlook Handbook. It is important that your match with the job be a "quality" match, both for your sake as well as the employer's sake. In your case, your career development and future hinges on every career decision and step you make. In the employer's case, thousands of dollars of money are spent to recruit, hire, orient, and train a new employee; that's a considerable investment that they do not want to "waste" on an unqualified and uncommitted candidate.

4. **Do you have evidence in your work history and training to prove that you possess the skills to do the job, and to do it well?** As you read the job posting and job description, underline or highlight the skills mentioned and keep track of them. Do you possess the majority of those skills? Which ones would you need to acquire? If the skills you are lacking are critical to the job, no matter how interested you are in the job, you will need to obtain those skills. Even for entry-level jobs, a modicum of experience (perhaps through internships or volunteer work or class projects) is critical to winning consideration over other candidates. Remember: Anyone can claim a skill; that does not mean you actually possess it and do it well. The proof of those skills is in your accomplishments, which you must be prepared to cite in your job search communications to substantiate the credibility of your pursuit of particular job targets.

Using this list of questions will assist you in pre-qualifying your suitability for certain jobs, which will in turn maximize your job search efforts. Conducting a well-researched, targeted job search campaign will enable you to more readily achieve your desired result of a job you can love!

Unprepared for the Big Job Fair

Job Seeker's Story

Susan had just graduated with a four-year degree and decided to attend the university-sponsored job fair. She arrived bright and early, dressed appropriately in a conservative suit and with several copies of her résumé printed on linen paper.

After reviewing the list of companies in attendance, she realized no one there was hiring English majors, so she decided to look around. When she saw a booth for a national bank, a light bulb went off in her head. She thought of her friend who worked at a bank. He had good benefits and paid vacations. She also thought about the summers she had spent managing a video store: She had provided customer service, cash handling, staff supervision, scheduling, and daily balancing. How could she miss?

Without hesitation she took a deep breath, pasted on a friendly smile, and approached the imposing HR representative standing in the booth. Bravely she spoke the simple words that would seal her fate, *"I'm interested in working for your company."* The professional company representative didn't blink an eye but responded with an equally simple question, "Why?"

Why? Why? Susan thought wildly about what this woman would want to hear, but she wasn't prepared for this! I mean, wasn't the company supposed to just look at her résumé, tell her where she might fit, and ask her about her experience to make sure she was qualified?

When nothing smart came to mind she realized she had two choices: speak the seemingly lame reason that was careening around in her brain like a ping pong ball, or run for the door.

Finally, she said the only thing she could squeeze from her frozen and terrified brain, *"For the money?"*

Seconds that seemed to last hours ticked by as the HR representative stared at Susan. Then the HR representative turned on her heel, walked behind the table in the booth, and with a crook of her finger, gestured for Susan to join her.

The next few moments passed in a blur as the HR representative instructed Susan at length to go home and not waste her own or a prospective employer's time again until she knew what she wanted to do and how she was qualified to do it. Susan then stumbled out to her car, all thoughts of visiting additional job fair booths lost in her desire to go home and hide under the covers of her bed.

Job Seeker's Stumble

Poor Susan thought the job fair represented a chance to talk casually to employers and learn more about them on the spot. Susan blundered by not:

> Learning what companies would be participating in the job fair in advance.

> Having a clear job target in mind first.

> Understanding that employers expect job seekers to be able to explain why they are qualified to work in their business/industry and to know something about their organizations.

Job Seeker's ≥New Strategy≤

The ticket to job fair success is to plan and prepare in advance. Specifically:

1. **Find out what companies are attending in advance.** Usu- ally advertisements list the specific companies, or, at mini- mum, the type of companies that will be in attendance. Once you know who is attending, you can visit the companies' Websites to see what type of positions for which they are currently hiring and see where you might fit.

2. **Be prepared to interview.** Job fairs are not a place where full interviews take place, but employers expect job seek- ers to be able to answer common questions such as: *"What kind of position are you looking for?" "Tell me a little about yourself,"* and occasionally, *"Why do you want to work here?"*

3. **Have a job target.** This type of knowledge will help you avoid being billed as a generalist. It is never a good idea to say, *"I'll do anything"* or *"I'm flexible."* Employers are in- terested in individuals who can fit specific positions versus the generalist jack-of-all-trades.

4. **Take a more proactive approach.** It's easy to approach a booth and say, *"Would you like a copy of my résumé?"* or *"Are you accepting applications? I have my résumé."* As you have most likely experienced, the HR representative will accept that résumé from you and move to the next person who is waiting, leaving you to wonder if it will ever be looked at again as it lands on the giant stack of applicants. Next time, do things a little bit differently:

   > Attend during lunch or early afternoon when it is less crowded and you can get face time with the company representatives.

   > Approach the booth prepared to talk. Introduce your- self and express that you are interested in determining if you have the type of skills the company seeks in a candi- date. Ask if the employer might have a moment to pro- vide you with feedback by taking a look at your résumé. If it is busy or he or she seems distracted, ask if you might leave the résumé with him or her, and follow up by phone later in the week.

Alternatively, if you know what the company is looking for, you can be even more proactive by stating, "*I understand your firm is currently seeking mechanical engineers. I have 10 years of experience, most recently with the XYZ company. I am wondering if you might have a moment to take a look at my résumé and let me know if I have the specific background that your company might be interested in.*"

With just a little effort, you can take charge of the job fair, make a positive lasting impression, and increase your chances of getting a call that leads to an interview.

Limiting Your Job Search Can Be a Dangerous Strategy
Job Seeker's Story

Knowing that a major company restructuring was underway due to a merger, Marc and his fellow employees often discussed their job situations and wondered who would remain and who would be laid off. Because Marc was bored with his Information Technology (IT) position, which he had held for nine years with this major food distributor, he actually welcomed the opportunity to look elsewhere for employment. Almost immediately Marc discovered an IT job opening through his networking contacts at a small, 45-person technology company. Marc applied and was granted an interview.

Marc's interview went well and the feedback he got from the HR department was very positive. Consequently, two weeks later Marc was asked back to interview with the head of the IT Department. That interview proved to be even more positive and exciting for Marc. He was intrigued by the start-up technology challenges the company faced as it was growing, and the IT Director acknowledged that Marc had just the right mix of qualifications for the job.

As Marc went through these interviews, he procrastinated about searching for any other job leads or openings. After all, it seemed the company he had interviewed with would surely make a job offer based on his stellar interviews with HR and the IT Director.

After two more weeks passed, Marc was invited in for an interview with the CEO. Because it was a small, start-up company the CEO wanted to meet him, and Marc thought this interview would clinch the deal for the new job. Marc impressed the CEO with his enthusiasm, breadth of knowledge, and team spirit. Another week went by before Marc heard back from the CEO indicating that they had decided to postpone hiring for the new position until more customers were secured and the business base was stronger. Marc was very disappointed; he really had liked the people, the company culture, and the work environment. This perceived rejection caused Marc to put off his job search.

As luck would have it, one month later the company called again. They asked Marc to re-interview for the new position with representatives from the IT team in one week. This time Marc expected a job offer after his interview, so he gladly went to the interview and, aglow with confidence, won over his prospective new teammates. Ten days later Marc received a letter saying that a hiring freeze had been instituted and the company regretted that his application was put "on hold."

Marc again went into a tailspin of depression and loss of confidence. As he continued to work at his current job, he saw many of his colleagues being downsized and wondered if he would be next. It seemed too remote a possibility, especially because he did his job so well. His performance reviews had always been "above average," so he felt that would insulate him from being cut from the team.

Six weeks after his last interview with the start-up company, the incumbent CEO (with whom Marc had interviewed) stepped down and a new CEO came on board. During the leadership transition, the new CEO implemented departmental changes, including hiring a new IT Director, and lifted the hiring freeze. The new IT Director almost immediately invited Marc back, yet again, for another interview. Positive a job offer was just an interview away, Marc happily accepted. The new IT Director had been lured away from a competitor company and Marc was impressed with his ideas for rejuvenating the IT department. Likewise, the IT Director was impressed with Marc's technical abilities, interpersonal skills, and leadership potential.

Because the new CEO had not yet met Marc, the IT Director arranged an interview for Marc with him the following week. The new CEO seemed busy and distracted during the interview, which ended abruptly after only a half hour. Because the new CEO had replaced key members of the IT team, he did want Marc to interview with the new team—a step he called a "mere formality." That interview took another three weeks to arrange due to conflicting schedules and projects of the team members. In the meantime, Marc was buoyed up by the thought that his prospects had certainly taken a turn for the better. He felt sure that within a week after this next interview with the new team he would be made an excellent job offer and hired.

However, the odyssey of Marc's experiences with this company was not yet at an end. Although many on the 10-member interview panel of the IT team were the same people Marc had impressed in his previous interview, two new people on the team were skeptical of Marc's ability to fit into the now more aggressive and fast-paced company culture. They kept asking him for instances in which he had quickly adapted to changing project demands and how he had kept projects moving forward when there seemingly was little momentum or drive from other team members. Marc could not think of any examples to cite. As the interview progressed, Marc became more confused and dejected. He could not understand what was happening.

After all, this interview was supposed to be a "mere formality"; the job offer was supposed to be imminent.

Unfortunately, after more than five months and seven interviews with the start-up company, Marc did not receive a job offer. Less than two weeks later, Marc was downsized from this current job and he knew he had to begin his job search anew. But, feeling discouraged and depleted of energy, Marc was at a loss about how he would be able to do that.

Job Seeker's Stumble

Marc's ongoing interview saga with the start-up company and the accompanying roller-coaster of emotions he felt could have been ameliorated had Marc not "put all his eggs in one basket." Doing so limited his job-search possibilities to a great extent and left him vulnerable to outside forces over which he had no control. All of the effort and energy Marc had put into the seven rounds of interviews, combined with his high expectations, had resulted in job-search–crippling feelings including loss of self-worth, inertia, and depression.

Job Seeker's ≥New Strategy≤

Enduring and thriving during a job search, which can typically extend from many weeks to many months, is critical to shortening the job search process while at the same time enabling you to secure an enjoyable and financially rewarding job. The following basic strategies will aid you in this endeavor:

▷ **Never Limit Your Job Search to Only One Job Opening:** Keep your job search pipeline filled with job leads by using a wide variety of job search methods, such as online and offline networking, employee referrals, online job boards and niche boards, direct contact with targeted companies, want ads in newspapers and trade journals, recruiters and staffing agencies, and job fairs. Even if you have a "promising" interview, continue to job search anyway. In this way you can maximize your control over the ultimate outcome—finding a good job that really interests you—because you will have generated enough quality leads, rather than relying on just one or two leads. You may also find that this approach produces multiple job offers simultaneously!

▷ **Prepare a Job Search Plan—Then Do It!** One of the best ways to positively impact your job search is to gain control through planning and organizing a job search action plan. Taking the time to attend to the overall strategy of your job search, and then breaking that strategy down into manageable "chunks" will make an oftentimes overwhelming goal of attaining a new job seem much more doable. Be sure to include an information-management system with your job search activities, such as an Excel spreadsheet or the advanced career-management tool set at JibberJobber.

▷ **Establish a Support Network:** You will find that the support of positive-minded people can serve to buoy you up when you feel down, and help you keep perspective on your life and job search. Besides a support system of family and friends, joining a job search group (sometimes called "job clubs") will allow you to expand your network, which in turn can reveal new job opportunities. Even more, by helping others in the group with job leads and networking contacts, you will be focusing on someone else besides yourself. That can be a healthy break from self-absorption and potential job-search isolation.

▷ **Nurture Yourself:** Meeting your life-balance needs on all levels, such as physical, mental, emotional, and spiritual, will allow you to remain in your "center of calmness" and avoid the wild, roller-coaster swings of emotion that can cripple job-search progress. Taking care of yourself with a well-balanced diet, hobbies you enjoy, and daily physical exercise are especially helpful in modulating serotonin levels, which can contribute to a sense of well-being.

▷ **Make a Medical Evaluation Part of Your Plan:** Because a job search can be stressful, it's important to have your health evaluated regularly. Doing so can enable the diagnosis and early treatment of illnesses, both physical and emotional, that can be obstacles to a shorter, more successful job search process.

Follow Up With Courtesy and Class

Job Seeker's Story

Martha had been a senior member of the Human Resources staff for a major retailer for six years. During that time she developed a growing pet peeve based on a regular occurrence she experienced with job applicants. It seemed that not a day would go by that an applicant was not calling and demanding to know why he or she had not heard back about the position. Martha found their demanding attitudes unbelievable because, in almost all the cases, the individual had been called already but did not have an answering machine, his or her phone was busy, or a message was left and had obviously not been received by the applicant.

Though Martha would be courteous and professional on the phone with each caller, she would always mark the application to reflect that he or she was not to be contacted again after the negative impression he or she made. She further stressed to her fellow staff that each applicant was to receive only one call and then was to be put at the bottom of the stack of applicants. This was necessary because of the high volume of applicants the company received.

Job Seeker's Stumble

Displaying an unprofessional attitude, exasperation, and/ or frustration with a company representative will always result in immediate termination of a job seeker's consideration for employment. If you display these negative personality traits early on, you are just helping the company to avoid making the mistake of hiring you and having you act that way as an employee.

Further, the job seeker is responsible for having adequate technology or plans in place to make sure that an employer's call can successfully be received and recorded.

Job Seeker's ≷New Strategy≷

You should always remember that, just because you are not speaking to the person who would be your supervisor, the individual you are talking to will have an impact on your future with the company. Company staff at all levels discuss applicants, and they look for warning signs such as disrespect toward staff members whom the job seeker might feel are below him or her in the hiring process. If you are rude or your voice simply sounds cold or abrupt over the phone, you could ruin your chances with the company. To avoid having this happen to you, take a few simple steps:

▷ **Wear a Smile:** Studies have shown that if you have a smile on your face you will sound more upbeat and positive. The best way to accomplish this is to practice with a mirror next to the phone.

▷ **Never Let Them See You Sweat:** You can easily convey displeasure, frustration, or irritation by how loudly you speak, how fast you talk, or the tone you inflect. Therefore, it is important to stay positive and aware of how you sound at all times.

▷ **Expect the Best Outcome:** Enter into every employer communication with the belief that everything will work out. If you expect the best you will be more apt to come across as proactive and upbeat.

▷ **Have an Answering System in Place:** Employers are busy professionals who do not (and will not) have the time to call you repeatedly. Invest in voice mail or a recorder, as well as call waiting, to make it easier for an employer to reach you. If you live with family or roommates who will not give you the message, consider using a cell phone number only or temporarily installing a ring master second phone line that goes straight to a private voice mail.

By positioning yourself as a professional, making it easy for an employer to reach you, and showing courtesy for company representatives, you will increase your chances of coming out on top in your job search!

Establish a Support System That Works for You

Job Seeker's Story

Shanelle had been a stay-at-home mom for seven years, raising her two daughters with her husband, and was actively involved in school and church activities. Shanelle needed to get back into the job market and had decided for expediency reasons to pursue the same types of jobs she had before leaving the workforce (as an Administrative Assistant and Executive Assistant). Shanelle's husband, Tyler, an agricultural economist, promised to support Shanelle throughout her job search by taking care of their two girls in the evenings and on weekends. That way, Shanelle could have some "free time" to devote to job search activities.

With this plan in place, Shanelle began to discover that much of her "free time" for job search was eroded with constant questions from Tyler about how to manage the girls' evening and weekend activities, and chores. The girls struggled for her attention when she was supposed to researching job openings on the Internet. In desperation, Shanelle asked Tyler to take a day off from work so that she could have a full day

to concentrate on much-needed job search tasks. Tyler consented and the day started off well. As Shanelle was in the shower, a clearly agitated Tyler (with the two girls screaming in the background at the top of their lungs) burst into the bathroom and handed Shanelle the cordless phone, exclaiming, *"It's for you!"*

Astounded, Shanelle leaned out of the shower (so as not to get the phone wet) and was horrified to hear the voice of a Human Resources representative that she had left a message for on the previous day! Fumbling to turn off the shower so she could hear better and closing the bathroom door to minimize the background noise of shrieking children, Shanelle tried to calm herself. She hoped the HR person would be understanding, but was disappointed to hear her say, *"Obviously this is not a good time. I'll call you back."* In fact, there was no further contact from the company, and Shanelle was too embarrassed to call the HR representative to try to explain. She felt demoralized and inadequate to the task of continuing her job search.

Job Seeker's Stumble

Expecting her entire support system of one—her husband—to function smoothly without any guidance or ground rules in the first few weeks of her job search left Shanelle aggravated and distracted. Although sincere and well-meaning, Shanelle's husband was a novice in the job-search support role. Apparently, he was also a novice in the daily activities required to deal with two rambunctious children who missed the attention of their mother. Consequently, Shanelle's job search did not progress well. When she was finally contacted by a prospective company for what she hoped would turn into an interview, she experienced a total meltdown of her support system that jeopardized her self-esteem and job-search efforts.

Job Seeker's ≳New Strategy≲

Many job seekers find themselves lacking sufficient support to allow their job search activities to progress effectively and efficiently. As a mother re-entering the workforce after a seven-year gap of employment, Shanelle felt stressed enough with having to deal with the implications of that on her job search. In addition, her self-confidence about her career prospects was at an all-time low. The bulk of job seekers experience negative emotions and stress during a job search, just as Shanelle did. However, the degree of those negative emotions and the impact on one's job search can be reduced to a large extent by establishing and maintaining a fully functional support system and team. Here are some suggestions to do just that:

▷ **Start With a Well-Defined Goal:** Gain your support team's buy-in by including them in your job search plans. Start by pinpointing the ultimate goal—the kind of job you really want—and help your team understand the impact on them when you reach the goal. This will enable all of you to keep invested in and moving toward the goal.

▷ **Set Up a Daily and Weekly Job Search Plan:** Create a specific, measurable, and realistic job search plan with time frames for both daily and weekly activities. Your job search plan may include time for researching companies and industries, developing a marketing communications plan, writing self-marketing documents such as résumés and cover letters, identifying job leads and networking prospects, telephone calls, e-mail, information interviews, job interviews, attending job fairs, networking meetings, reading job search and career materials, documentation of job search activities and contacts, and transportation time to and from interviews, meetings, and job fairs. Remember to also include time to "unwind" from your job search by exercising, socializing, doing hobbies, and being with friends and family. Post your plan (both daily and weekly) where your support team can see it. This will encourage accountability on your part and keep everyone aware of what tasks are required every day to achieve the goal.

▷ **Secure Your Support Team:** Check out your entire network to recruit for regular and intermittent support-team members. Scrutinize your e-mail or PDA address book and holiday card-giving list for more possibilities beyond immediate family members and friends. In Shanelle's case, she would have discovered there were other return-to-work moms in her network who could have formed a job seeker support group. This group could have taken turns babysitting the children, which would have freed time for other moms in the group to conduct their job search unencumbered for the day.

▷ **Gather Resources:** Maximize your time, energy, and efforts by preparing the physical resources needed for an efficient job search. Obtain or borrow a good-quality printer and computer with Internet capability, word-processing, and information-management software; a cell phone (at minimum); an interviewing and job search meeting wardrobe; reliable transportation; résumé and cover letter paper and envelopes; a professional-looking portfolio for your marketing communications materials to take to an interview; and personal business cards.

▷ **Cope With Stress:** Be sure to arrange backup systems for your support team, computer, printer, telephone, and transportation, which are all vital to successfully conducting a worry-free job search. Mentally rehearse what you would do in the event of a breakdown in each of the resources listed here, and develop a clear plan for what you would do. Organize your time to do something each day that brings you joy and re-energizes you. Eliminate unnecessary distractions and commitments, and avoid energy-draining, negative people. Learn to delegate to your support team and trust that they will do fine. (You do not have to micro-manage them.) Smile and laugh more often, by yourself and with others. Do what is most important first. Take frequent breaks to relax. Get a massage. Maintain a healthy diet and exercise regime to generate more sustainable energy and even out mood swings. Seek out close friends or professional help if you feel unable to cope.

▷ **Adjust Your Job Search Plans:** Keep track of how you use your daily job search time and the results generated over one to two months. You will likely be amazed at the difference between how you think you use your time and what you actually do. Analyze to find the 20 percent of your activities that generate 80 percent of your results, and maximize your efforts and those of your support team by focusing on those activities. Do not eliminate activities that enable you to better cope with stress or that re-energize you; those are results you need in order to maintain the grueling pace of a job search.

▷ **Understand Your "Personal Style":** Identify how and when you work best, as well as the barriers that are preventing you from realizing the productivity you desire. Get feedback from those on your support team, including close friends and family members. Ask them to help you identify the aspects of your personal style that are hindering your job search efforts.

▷ **Stay Flexible:** Your daily and weekly priorities will change as your job search moves along. Re-assess your weekly mini-goals to better allocate your time and support-system resources. Step back from your activities periodically and ask yourself, *"Is what I am doing right now moving me* *closer to my mini-goal for the week? Would my support team agree this is moving me closer to reaching the goal?"*

There are many ways your support system and team can maximize your job search return on investment for time and energy provided you establish guidelines, structures, and suggestions for their support. Make use of your support team wisely, and the payback for everyone will be a much shorter search!

Résumé for Many Different Job Targets = No Response
Job Seeker's Story

Dori had worked for three years in an entry-level customer service support job right out of college and had recently gotten a promotion to Customer Service Manager. Unfortunately, there was no significant pay raise with that promotion. Dori worked as a Manager for another three months, but then felt she was ready to move on to something different. But what? She had liked dealing with the Human Resources department in her company and it seemed like interesting work, especially coaching and training employees. On the other hand, friends of hers had mentioned that being a pharmaceutical sales representative was really lucrative. Dori was also drawn to a job in the outdoors, such as a Park Ranger or Forest Ranger. Although she did not have any experience or training in any of these kinds of jobs, Dori felt she could learn them quickly.

Dori crafted a one-page, reverse chronological résumé with her education, work history, and dates of employment. To fill up the page, she included part-time jobs she held as a waitress and theme-park attendant, in addition to her full-time positions as a Customer Service Representative and Customer Service Manager. Dori left her Objective statement blank, figuring she could fill it in with a job title in response to whatever job posting caught her eye. This seemed an easy strategy that still would make it appear that her résumé was "targeted" for a particular job.

The first three jobs Dori applied for included Human Resources Manager (at her current company, which was hiring for that position), as well as Pharmaceutical Sales Representative, and Forest Ranger. As Dori customized her résumé with the specific job title for each opening, she felt confident that she would obtain interviews very soon. After all, she thought, given the vast array of jobs listed online, it should be an easy task to send out one hundred résumés in a month, which in turn should yield many, many interviews and job offers.

Dori followed this strategy for two months, applying for a diverse cross-section of occupations, none of which were in customer service. Each time she tailored the Objective with the job title in the job posting and submitted it online. She was incredulous that she had not yet gotten one interview. In fact, she had not gotten one response!

Job Seeker's Stumble

What Dori created was a generic résumé with a slight nod to "customization" by including the job title from the online job posting. Generic résumés typically provide a "laundry list" of information such as jobs held, with accompanying dates in reverse chronological order, along with education attained, and a vague Objective. In this way, the job seeker hopes to "keep my options open." This generic approach to résumé writing used to be the norm 20 years ago when Human Resources staff might have perused a résumé to establish a fit with an open position. That is no longer the case. Dori's mistake consisted of assuming such a "listing" constituted a powerful, up-to-date approach to résumé writing. It did not.

Job Seeker's New Strategy

Employers expect that candidates have sifted through various career possibilities, have defined a career focus, and have applied for a job opening because it matches their career focus. Employers do not want to be career counselors for applicants by attempting to make a "match" for them. Their task of re-cruiting and hiring quality talent is already stressed by the vol-ume of résumés they receive for every open position—often hundreds, if not thousands, of résumés. Consequently, the employment reviewer's impetus is to screen out, rather than screen in, applicants based on two obvious criteria: credibil-ity and distinctiveness. This requires job seekers to take a more substantive approach in crafting their résumés than simply "customizing" an Objective statement. Let's examine each of the two basic criteria:

▷ **Credibility:** The résumé, in effect, needs to market the job seeker for a particular position by establishing proof that the job seeker should be considered a credible candi-date by the employment reviewer. The minimum bar for credibility is established by the employer, and is often listed as "Job Requirements." So, as you peruse the require-ments in a job posting and find required items (such as certain college degrees, licenses, certifications, technol-ogy skills, and experience), understand that these are the credibility builders that must appear in your résumé. If, as is the case with Dori, you have no training or experi-ence in an occupational field, it is unlikely that an em-ployment reviewer would consider you a credible candidate. Note that there are some instances in which generic résumés might be sufficient, such as job postings for which no requirements or minimal requirements are mentioned. These are often entry-level jobs or "revolving-door" jobs (where newly hired employees come and go so quickly the employer needs to keep a constant stream of applicants in the pipeline).

▷ **Distinctiveness:** After your résumé has passed the cred-ibility hurdle, the next hurdle has to do with what makes you unique. In other words, why should the employment reviewer call you in for an interview versus someone else who possesses similar credibility factors? Your résumé can potentially stand out in diverse ways, but two of the best methods are through accomplishments (what you have been able to produce of value in previous jobs) and through personal branding (how you were able to produce those accomplishments). Top-notch accomplishments tell meaningful stories and showcase benefits to the employer, such as making money, saving money, cutting costs, bringing in new customers, or retaining loyal customers who continue to buy products and services. Accomplishments such as these grab the employment reviewer's attention and separate you from the bulk of candidates who simply copy job duties and responsibilities from their job descriptions.

To further refine your distinctiveness and narrow your field of competition, include mention of your personal-branding style. The attributes you are known for and the manner in which you achieve your accomplishments are uniquely your own. Highlight your personal brand, and the employment reviewer will begin to "see" you fitting into the job and the company culture before you have even had your first interview. For more on personal branding, including a personal-branding quiz, go to the Assessment Goddess—Personal Branding Quiz (*www.assessmentgoddess.com/brandingquiz.html*).

Generic résumés are easy to spot because they lack credibility and distinctiveness. They appear mass-produced and unfocused. Why would an employment reviewer consider an applicant with that approach to be a quality match and a prime candidate for an interview? Take some time to find and prove the "quality match" between you and a job opening in your résumé; you may then find an employment reviewer will recognize that match based in credibility and distinctiveness and put you at the top of his or her "to be interviewed" list!

Have a Script for Responding to Job Ads

Job Seeker's Story

Tonya responded to an advertisement she saw for an Instructor at the Business Institute of America. When she called she reached a voice-mail system that asked her to leave a message. Her message went as follows:

"Yes, my name is Tonya <Last Name> and I think I am a good match for the position you advertised in the Sun Times. *I have been a teacher for 17 years and have taught subjects such as math, English, science, history, foreign languages, economics, and customer service. I really love working with people and teaching, and know I can make a good contribution to your school. I am hardworking, professional, and very interested in being considered. Thank you."*

Once Tonya hung up she realized she never provided her phone number. She called back and left a hurried message stating she had called before and was not sure she had left her phone number. This time she provided her phone number, apologized, and then added that she was the one with 17 years experience.

Hanging up, Tonya was frustrated with herself as well as with the company for not having someone live to take applicant calls. Tonya did not receive a call for an interview.

Job Seeker's Stumble

At first glance the mistake here is simply that she had to call twice and seemed unprepared. However, those are only two of the mistakes Tonya made with her call. Statements such as *"I think I am a good match..."* would leave the employer feeling as if she was not sure herself of her match. Additionally, her message was repetitive, with *good* being said in two consecutive sentences. Also, her message did not present any unique selling propositions to help her stand out from the other applicants that would make an employer feel he needed to speak to her for this position. Finally, she assumed the company was only hiring for one position when she left her message.

Job Seeker's ≥New Strategy≤

Before you pick up the phone to call an employer, it is a good idea to have a brief script written out of what you would like to say. That way, you can be assured that you will not ramble, will not leave out pertinent information (such as your phone number), and will have the opportunity to express your unique strengths and talents for the position. A typical script might look this way:

My name is _____, and my phone number is _____. I am responding to your advertisement in the <Paper Name/Website Name> for a <Job Title>. I am confident that I can be an asset to the position and your organization because of

_____, _____, and _____. Further, my strengths and achievements in _____ will be an asset. I would appreciate the opportunity to meet with you and discuss your needs and my qualifications. Again, my name is _____ and my phone number is _____.

When you craft your message, strive to emphasize your unique strengths and qualifications for the position. Read it out loud a few times to make sure it sounds natural, and make adjustments as needed.

As you leave your message, be sure to speak slowly and clearly while keeping a smile on your face and an upbeat tone to your voice. Additionally, you might want to spell your name at the end to make sure the employer writes it down correctly. Your message may sound similar to this:

"Good afternoon, my name is Tonya <Last Name>, and I am a certified trainer with over 10 years of expertise in delivering dynamic adult training. I am extremely interested in applying my experience in business instruction at the university and business school level to the Instructor position that you advertised in the Sun Times. *I would appreciate the opportunity to meet with you so that I can introduce you to some of the award-winning curriculum that I have developed as well as the student and organizational critiques I have received from Fortune 500 companies on my training programs. Again, my name is Tonya <Last Name>. That's T-o-n-y-a <Last Name Spelled Out>, and my phone number is 555-555-1212. I look forward to speaking with you soon. Thank you."*

Notice the difference in Tonya's message now? There are no weasel words or phrases such as *good* and *I think,* and the content is not thin, repetitive, or abbreviated to miss unique selling propositions or her phone number. By carefully creating a dynamic, professional, and results-focused message, you can also leave a professional impression on the prospective employer.

Early Bird Gets the Worm

Job Seeker's Story

Christopher found a position listed on an Internet job board after it had been posted for several weeks. It was late on Friday afternoon, and, because he assumed the listing might be about to end, he submitted his résumé and went out to meet friends for dinner. Dinner turned into drinks, and drinks turned into a late night on the town.

The next day Christopher slept late and had breakfast while reading the paper. He picked up the phone at 1:00 p.m. to make a call and realized he had a message. The message was from 5:30 p.m. the day before and had been left by the employer he had contacted with his résumé. Mr. Arkin had asked him to return the call as soon as possible.

Christopher picked up the phone and called the employer, even though it was Saturday. They spoke for approximately 20 minutes and had a wonderful conversation in which they both acknowledged what a perfect match Christopher would be for the position. Christopher was thrilled to get the chance to speak with him.

However, Mr. Arkin then explained that he had hoped to speak to Christopher the evening before or that morning, as he had scheduled a second interview with a candidate at 11:00 a.m. and had just finished making her an offer. He told Christopher that he would love to consider him but would have to wait and see what came of the offer he extended. Of course Christopher could do nothing but thank him and tell him he looked forwarded to hopefully hearing from him soon.

Unfortunately, Christopher was notified the following week that the other candidate had accepted the position.

Job Seeker's Stumble

Christopher was unaware that once you enter a job search that you should be checking your phone messages (or e-mail, if that is how you applied) regularly to ensure you can get back to a prospective employer immediately.

Job Seeker's ≳New Strategy≲

Think of your job search as a race where everyone is striving to get to the finish line first. If you are not there to take the call/return the call or respond to the e-mail in a timely manner, another job seeker could do so first and capture the employer's interest. Quite often the old adage about the early bird getting the worm is true when it comes to hiring.

The best way to ensure you can respond in a timely manner is to:

▹ Check your voice-mail messages in the morning, just before lunch (so you can return a call at lunchtime), in mid-afternoon (so you can return a call before the end of business), and once in the evening.

▷ Be careful about screening phone calls, because employers can call in the evening and could show up on caller identification as "unknown name" or "unavailable." Do not assume these are sales calls, as they could be prospective employers.

▷ Always answer the phone professionally. An employer will not understand if you answer the phone half-asleep in the middle of the day, or with loud music or screaming voices in the background. If you cannot control your surroundings or act professional, positive, and upbeat, you are better off not answering and returning the call a little later.

▷ Prepare family who might be answering the phone to answer the phone professionally and to take detailed, accurate messages.

Similar rules for timely follow-up apply to e-mail, so be vigilant, especially if it is typical for you to only check your e-mail periodically.

Through timely follow-up you can stay ahead of the competition and win the race to get the job.

CHAPTER 6

Networking Nightmares

∧

Don't Let Your Hot Leads Go Cold!

Job Seeker's Story

With a new bachelor's degree in marketing and communications, James was eager to begin his job search, because he really felt his calling was in persuasive communications. But James was also a bit anxious. He had changed careers from the Human Resources field and felt he might have some difficulty explaining his career transition to potential employers.

Due to this anxiety, James sought out a career coach, Melissa, to assist him developing a job search strategy and communications pieces to better position him as a job and career changer. Melissa advised him to begin with some informational interviewing in Marketing and Communications for potential job leads and to build his self-confidence within that field.

In fact, Melissa referred James to the Vice President of Marketing and Communications for a statewide professional association. Melissa told James she had contacted the VP, who agreed to take James's call. The VP had also started out originally in Human Resources, and felt she had a lot to share with James about how to successfully market himself. Melissa coached James about informational interview goals and possible questions to ask. In addition, she agreed to invite James to join her LinkedIn network, which at the time included 1.5 million people among the three levels of her network, so he could begin to explore possible marketing and communications resources and leads.

A few weeks later, Melissa saw the VP at a professional meeting and asked if James had contacted her. He had not, which was particularly sad, because the VP had a strong job lead for an immediate opening in corporate marketing communications that paid very well. Then Melissa remembered that James had not accepted her LinkedIn invitation, even though he had agreed to do so in their coaching session. Melissa called and then e-mailed James twice that week and left messages, but did not hear back from him. A few months later, Melissa ran into James at the local bank, where he had an entry-level position as a bank teller.

Job Seeker's Stumble

James did many things right. He completed a degree program in a field that held strong interest and was a good match for his strengths, and he sought out the professional advice of a career coach to help him overcome his job search anxiety. However, James's lack of follow-through on an informational interview referral cost him a "hot" job lead in his field. This simple oversight, combined with dropping "warm leads" through his career coach's networking connections on LinkedIn, contributed to a stalled job search, and, ultimately, his decision to interview for and accept an entry-level job posted in the local newspaper.

Job Seeker's New Strategy

The solution for this misstep seems easy enough: follow through on each and every lead as soon as possible, because that one lead might develop into the job of your dreams. However, assiduously meeting that goal can get sidetracked by non-productive human behavior. Some of these common behavioral obstacles include:

▷ **Procrastination:** Call or e-mail within 24 hours of receiving the lead. At the very least you can use that initial communication to set up a time to talk in more depth. Do not let your "hot" lead grow cold!

▷ **Lack of Time Management:** If you are networking well, you may find you are getting so many job leads or contacts for informational interviews that you feel deluged. Before you get to this stage, create some "template" e-mails that you can quickly customize for the initial introduction, the follow-up to setting the appointment with the referral, and the thank-you after the meeting. Remember to ask your referral in the first communication whether he or she prefers to be contacted by telephone or e-mail, and then stay in touch using that method. Commit to following up with a set number of leads per day; carve out time from your day to do this absolutely necessary networking step. No one else will follow up for you.

▷ **Lack of Organization:** Beyond creating customizable "template" e-mails, organize your communications into desktop folders by type for easy and logical access. You may want to develop a spreadsheet or "tickler" file system to remind you of follow-up dates for e-mails. With an online career-management system such as JibberJobber, you can import your contacts, set up e-mails to notify yourself of follow-ups you need to do, store e-mail communications, and more.

▷ **Lack of Self-Confidence and Personal Courage:** Shyness and anxiety about networking and follow-up are actually very common. In fact, the very people you may want to network with could be just as shy about networking themselves! Start by desensitizing yourself to the networking situation; network with friends, acquaintances, and family members whom you can trust to be helpful. Always be prepared with good questions to ask, and rehearse them ahead of time. Listen more than you talk, and take notes. You want to capture really important information without getting it distorted, and you certainly want to get names and contact information accurately for follow-up. You can also attend meetings of Toastmasters International to develop your one-on-one and public speaking skills and self-confidence.

▷ **Premature or Ill-Advised Decision-Making:** The impulse to shorten your job search by taking the first reasonable job that comes along is difficult to overcome. After all, who wants to be in a long, drawn-out job search? Who wants to face possible rejection every day? Try to remember that the pay-off for persistence in the face of rejection is like mining for gold: The really great job—the job of your dreams—could be just one lead away. Also, typically the informational interviews that result in great job leads are not usually with the first level of people you see, but rather with the people they refer you to.

▷ **Inactivity:** Networking has long been the number-one way people find jobs. But the reality is that no one is going to do it for you. Consistency is the key; commit to networking, devise a workable plan for you, and then make a commitment to yourself to work your plan every day. Without commitment to act, the best plans mean nothing.

Give Before You Can Get for Networking Success
Job Seeker's Story

Betty was excited to attend her first business networking event and was sure she would leave with many referrals and opportunities. As soon as she arrived she began walking from person to person reciting her 10-second introduction.

She said to each person she approached, *"Hi. I am Betty Johnson; I am a civil rights attorney with 15 years' experience. I specialize in disability cases. Do you know anyone that can use my services?"* Once completed, she flashed a smile and handed over a business card.

It did not matter if the individuals she approached were in conversation already; Betty barged into one-on-one conversations and small groups, never even waiting for natural breaks in chats to start her rehearsed speech. Betty never asked any questions of those she approached, never tried to understand how she might be able to help them, never asked others for their business cards, and never once waited around to see if the person/group to whom she was speaking had anything valuable to offer. She only introduced herself, anxiously listened as others tried to introduce themselves, and then moved on to the next person or group as soon as possible.

Betty left, feeling empowered because she had reached so many people in such a short time to let them know of her business. However, at the same time, she felt confused. Though she was sure she was doing what she was supposed to do in networking, it seemed that everyone was talking about her and might have even been laughing at her. *"Well, that's what networking is,"* she told herself. *"Getting the message out."* She believed she had done her best, so she returned home expecting the phone to ring.

Unfortunately, Betty did not receive any calls, nor did she follow up with any of the people she had met. She was frustrated by the time and effort she had wasted with networking. She opted not to attend any further meetings, dismissing them as a waste of precious time.

Job Seeker's Stumble

Although Betty made numerous mistakes in her networking, her greatest error was not just about what she could take from the experience, but what she should have given back as well. She should have shifted her approach from "what's in it for me?" to "what can I do for other people so that they'll remember me and want to help me?" At the end of the day, people only want to help those who are sincerely interested in them or whom they at least respect as an equal professional.

Job Seeker's ≥New Strategy≤

In order to succeed at networking, the best strategy is to focus on developing relationships that are long-lasting, giving, and mutually beneficial. When you meet new people, you will want to find out who they are, what they do, and what they want/need. Think about how you can help each person to reach his or her professional goals. You can do this successfully by:

> Asking what an ideal referral is for each person with whom you network.

> Talking with each person about his or her offerings so you know exactly what he or she does.

> Thinking about who you know who might benefit from his or her services or experience.

> Identifying and providing him or her with resources (such as news clippings and relevant Websites that you find) that he or she will find helpful.

> Keeping networking contacts warm through regular follow-up.

Likewise, when giving information about yourself, be open about your needs, but be sure to frame your information in a way that will benefit others.

By putting the needs of others before your own, you will come across as someone who is truly worth the time and effort of becoming a networking contact. Plus, you will become a resource people will want to know. This is a huge benefit of effective networking and will pay off through a lifetime of referrals. Remember that not every meeting is going to lead to a great relationship, but the golden rule of networking is giving before you get.

Speak Up to Stand Out

Job Seeker's Story

Sharla's friends at the telecommunications company where she had worked were concerned about her. It had been more than 10 months since she was laid off, and Sharla had devoted her entire job search time pursuing job postings on the Internet. Her two friends, Maggie and Iris (both in Marketing), had just been let go last week from the same telecom company.

Maggie and Iris asked Sharla if she would like to join them at a networking event for job seekers at a local church. It met every week, and they had heard good reports about the success of participants in securing job leads and interviews. Even though she knew she had to do something more productive regarding her job search, Sharla was reluctant. Communicating with others, particularly strangers, and face to face, was difficult. Sharla was shy and had not developed well-honed social skills. In fact, her chosen field of project management had afforded her the opportunity to communicate primarily via e-mail and reports.

At her friends' urging, Sharla attended the networking event and followed them around for the first half hour as they mingled. Maggie and Iris seemed to make connections easily, and always included Sharla in the introductions. But Sharla was at a loss after the introduction; what should she say? Even though she was among a group of other unemployed professionals, Sharla was embarrassed about her loss of a job (the first time this had ever happened to her). How could she explain that when anyone asked?

Sharla spent the next hour in a confused and miserable state. A few people came up to her and introduced themselves, handed out business cards, and promised to follow up with

Sharla the next day, but she wasn't too hopeful about that. She noticed that they quickly moved on to network with others after their brief conversation with her. Miraculously, her two friends managed to secure business cards and job leads from several attendees.

Sharla never did get any networking calls the next day. Dejected, she refused to go to the job seekers' networking group the following week with Maggie and Iris. She really could not understand their excitement. What Sharla did not know was that Maggie and Iris got phone interviews as a result of their leads, and Maggie was scheduled for a face-to-face interview in three days for a Marketing Director job that had not been advertised and needed to be filled immediately.

Job Seeker's Stumble

Using shyness as her "comfort blanket" insulated Sharla from trying to make social interactions, whether at work or at a networking meeting for job seekers. Unfortunately, feeling "safe" from communicating with others by avoiding them also meant Sharla was avoiding the use of a highly effective job search tool. Over the past several decades, networking has always been cited as the number-one method for obtaining viable job leads that result in interviews.

Job Seeker's ≥New Strategy≤

First, if you are embarrassed about being unemployed, you must learn to get over it. With the world of work being what it is, everyone you meet either has been or currently is unemployed. It's really not unusual anymore. According to the Bureau of Labor Statistics, workers change jobs about every four years on average; if you are under the age of 25, it ranges from six to 16 months!

At a job seeker networking event you will likely be interacting with a roomful of people who are all unemployed for various reasons. Do not apologize or try to "explain away" your situation. None of your fellow unemployed job seekers care how you came to be in the same networking event with them. What they do care about is how you can be of help to each other.

So what if you are shy? Many who are shy think that networking could not work for them, but it can! You might be an individual of few words, so think about going to a networking event with a buddy where you can take turns introducing each other. Sometimes talking about someone else (your buddy) is a lot easier than talking about yourself.

Be sure you and your networking buddy work out a plan ahead of time for what to say. You could even create a bullet-point outline (in large typeface on a 3 × 5 note card) and refer to it as your "cheat sheet." Besides the obvious introduction, try to come up with a succinct "elevator pitch" that makes clear your target ideal job—occupational field, level of position, and industry—and three compelling "value" points (backed up with concrete accomplishments) that make you unique and memorable.

Then, practice your introductions with friends and acquaintances before approaching strangers at a networking event. As you become more comfortable making the elevator pitch for your buddy, switch over now and then to your own introduction as your buddy listens. Ask for feedback after the event, so, even if you feel you "failed," you can experiment with new approaches at the next networking opportunity. In fact, you may want to consider joining your local chapter of Toastmasters with your networking buddy to speed up the process of becoming more polished and socially aware speakers.

At the very least, think about joining a small group at the networking meeting where you can listen, introduce yourself, and exchange personal business cards. Then, you can follow up after the event by sending an e-mail or handwritten note to let each person know what a pleasure it was to meet him or her and how you look forward to the next event, while also asking how you can be of help to him or her. When you spark a more thoughtful dialogue by offering assistance, you will be remembered. That means at the next networking meeting, you will most likely be introduced to more people whom you can add to your network via the same method.

Think of the 80/20 rule always: Talk about yourself 20 percent of the time so your listener understands who you are, what you need, and how he or she might be of assistance. The rest of the time (80 percent), ask good questions that show interest in others, and then listen. By establishing a connection of trust through sincere listening you will gain quality in networking contacts, not just quantity, from people who will become invested in your job search, just as you will become invested in theirs.

Whether your preferred networking style is face-to-face, or via e-mail or note, you can still accomplish your networking goals of building relationships that expand the "net" of just the right job leads you need. While you are working on overcoming your shyness in face-to-face situations, use social networks such as LinkedIn, Facebook, and MySpace (the top three social networks in terms of size) to establish a professional presence. Create a custom profile that contains the elements of your elevator pitch, as well as your career highlights, and then begin reaching out to your online network for information about target occupations, industries, and companies. Remember the 80/20 rule: Relationship etiquette means always reciprocating by asking how you can help the other person. You may come across leads for just the type of position others are seeking, or perhaps for someone in their family or a close friend. LinkedIn provides an easy vehicle for showing reciprocity through its Q&A feature; members put questions out to the LinkedIn community that anyone can answer. This is a powerful way to begin to draw new people into your network and build visibility.

Of course, you will want to follow up on all your generated leads. Do not pre-judge who is worthy of follow-up or not. You do not know the reach of others' networks, so follow up with everyone. You might even ask your networking contacts to make initial introductions for you to their referrals. This "warm lead" approach will let you know that referrals are expecting your call or e-mail, and are ready and willing to listen to you. Keep track of your contact and referral information using a contact database system such as JibberJobber. Be sure to include what your contacts and referrals need from you, topics/job leads/industries they are interested in, what you promised to do for them and by what date, what they promised to do for you, and then the follow-up steps you took, including thank-you notes. High-quality, "warm" contacts that you develop in this manner can become the networking basis for a lifetime!

Don't Overstay Your Welcome

Job Seeker's Story

Vince was incredibly interested in finding a networking contact within Xycom Industries, Inc. So when his colleague gave him the contact information for the VP of Marketing, Dan, Vince immediately gave him a call to discuss the possibility of meeting for a quick informational interview. He mentioned his colleague, and Dan agreed to meet the next day based on Vince's promise of just taking 15 minutes of his time.

When Vince and Dan met, the meeting was going quite positively and seemed on track, but when the 15 minutes were up, Vince showed no signs of stopping with his questions and chatting. Fifteen minutes turned into 25, and Dan began to look at his watch, and his phone was ringing. Yet Vince just kept on talking. Several times Dan tried to interrupt but Vince kept talking, blatantly ignoring the obvious signals Dan was sending.

Finally, Dan stood up and told Vince that he had another meeting and began to usher him out the door. Vince continued to chatter on until Dan was forced to interrupt him and tell him he was out of time. It still took another five minutes to get him out of the office. Vince was oblivious to how angry Dan had become at the abuse of his time.

Vince followed up with Dan several times for referrals and future networking opportunities, but he never received a return call.

Job Seeker's Stumble

Vince did not honor his agreement with Dan to only take 15 minutes of his time. By blatantly disregarding his promise, he showed disrespect and demonstrated that he was not a person who kept his word. He lost Dan's respect and willingness to assist him with his goal of employment by making a negative impression.

Job Seeker's ≷New Strategy≷

This is extremely simple: Always keep your promises, and do what you say you will do when you say you will do it. That's all it takes. People are busy, and, when they choose to gift you with some of their precious time—especially when they do not even know you—they deserve your respect. If you get in the door by promising to stay to 15 minutes, then that is what you should do.

In fact, when you arrive for your informational networking interview, you should reiterate that you promise to only take 15 minutes. If you find the individual you are meeting is very engaged in the conversation and that you are reaching your deadline, say, *"I promised to only take 15 minutes of your time, and, while I absolutely want to hear what you have to say, I know you are very busy. Do you have the extra time now to finish, or should we schedule another meeting at your convenience?"* If the individual is unaware of the time that has passed, he can reassess his available time; he will also respect you for not selfishly putting him behind in his day.

When the meeting is ending, be sure to ask for referrals to other people within the company. Send a thank-you card for the individual's time and information after the session, and follow up in approximately three days to see if he has thought of any additional referrals.

In the long run, you will get much more traction and results from your networking contacts if you respect their time.

Choose Your Networking Situations With Care

Job Seeker's Story

Jarrod was an enthusiastic and outgoing young college graduate with an eye on landing a sales position in surgical equipment sales. His bachelor's degree in communications certainly qualified him realistically for that field, and his self-confidence in making presentations had been rewarded in his courses with high grades and recognition from his professors. Unfortunately, Jarrod's fellow classmates were of a different opinion. They felt he was a bit overbearing, arrogant, and insensitive to others.

While partying in Fort Lauderdale, Florida, prior to beginning his job search, Jarrod fell and gashed his thigh. Because the bleeding was profuse and the gash required stitches, Jarrod was quickly taken to the nearest emergency room for medical care. As he lay being prepped for surgery, Jarrod remembered the "3-feet rule of networking," a precept drilled into him by his college's career counselor that stated that he should network with anyone within 3 feet. In fact, Jarrod always carried personal business cards with him just in case a good networking situation would arise. He thought, *This is great! What better place to network for a Surgical Equipment Sales position than in surgery?"*

As Jarrod pulled out one of his blood-stained business cards from his jeans, torn now and tossed to the side in the prep room, he looked expectantly into the eyes of the surgeon who entered the room and asked, *"Do you know of any job opportunities?"* The astounded surgeon was dumbstruck and put off by the timing of this inappropriate request.

Another job seeker, Elena, who had been laid off six months earlier as a Call Center Manager, approached visitors at her great-aunt's wake in a metropolitan funeral home, proffering her former company's business card. As Elena asked about openings for a Call Center Manager during the wake, one by one the visitors abruptly left without taking her card and shaking their heads in disbelief. Elena was disappointed that she could not obtain even one business card in return. As she left, Elena thought, *"So much for networking! There were so many people here for Aunt Gerri's funeral and not even one has a lead to a job for me!"*

Job Seeker's Stumble

Jarrod and Elena were both enthusiastic and certainly not shy about their networking endeavors. However, their lack of emotional intelligence in choosing appropriate situations for networking left their contacts feeling astounded, irritated, and unwilling to give either of them the time of day after the bad first impression both of them managed to convey.

Job Seeker's ≳New Strategy≲

These extreme examples both illustrate the importance of awareness of others' feelings in social situations that do not lend themselves to networking. Typically, these are highly emotionally charged events with urgent demands (emergency room) or of a negative nature (funeral). Neither of these circumstances is conducive to producing effective networking leads. Interestingly, if Jarrod or Elena had contacted these same people *after* the events rather than during it, they would probably have received a more positive response.

So, choose where and when to network with care. If your social or emotional intelligence (EQ) could use some ramping up, read about the subject. There are plenty of books about these topics. A search on Amazon for "emotional intelligence" revealed 9,300 items, and 13,600 items appeared for the topic of "social intelligence." In addition, ask for feedback from friends and acquaintances you know to be straightforward. Assure them that you are looking for honest feedback so you can enhance your social intelligence to better build relationships—for your job search and your life! Then listen and learn.

Learning when to network and how best to communicate with others is a skill every job seeker can improve. Networking opportunities abound, and, if used wisely, can be the number-one way to garner great job leads. Use the following list of networking groups to approach (both online and offline) as a start to building your own network. Specifically:

▷ **Personal groups** such as family, as well as current and former friends, neighbors, classmates, alumni, fraternity and sorority members, teachers and faculty members, guidance and career counselors and coaches, and pastors/ministers/spiritual advisors.

▷ **Job contacts** such as current and former employers, colleagues, supervisors, references, mentors and mentees, customers, clients, suppliers and vendors, and competitors.

▷ **Professional associations** for your occupation and/or industry where you can contact members, staff, speakers, and vendors/suppliers.

▷ **Service professionals** such as dentists, medical staff, insurance agents, real estate agents, bankers, caterers, and others who serve a diverse and large array of clients.

▷ **Community and volunteer groups** such as Kiwanis, Rotary, Elks, and Lions clubs, as well as church, school, and nonprofit groups.

▷ **Business groups** such as the chamber of commerce and Jaycees, for both your local community as well as the communities in which you are seeking employment.

▷ **Diversity/niche organizations** that are aligned with your personal characteristics and situation. These are particular to each person but could include groups based on gender, race, religion, sexual orientation, economic condition, hobbies and interests, and causes that you are passionate about and that constitute a core part of your psyche.

There are a multitude of individuals and groups with whom you could network. How you approach those potential contacts is critical. Understand what constitutes appropriate networking situations and the best etiquette for each one. Then watch how your initial best impression draws contacts into your network with ease!

CHAPTER 7

Common Job Curses

^

Dead-End Job Dilemma

Job Seeker's Story

Mary had a master's degree in music, but she felt she was in a job that was going nowhere. When she first started her job search right out of college, Mary did what everyone else seemed to be doing. She sent out hundreds of résumés, posted her résumé on job boards such as Monster and CareerBuilder, and searched the Internet for opportunities.

Two months later, after sending out 500 résumés, Mary got two replies, one interview, and one offer. It was not the job she really wanted, but she took it anyway. Five years and three jobs later, after sending out hundreds of résumés, Mary had a position as an Arts Manager—in title only. It was really an administrative support job. Mary was desperately unhappy and unfulfilled.

More than anything, Mary wanted a job that would make her feel energized and challenged—a job where she could actually use her music education and training. Mary wanted to feel valued and valuable. Attempting to advance her career, Mary reverted to her usual job-search mode: She sent out a hundred résumés (more or less) in response diverse Internet job postings and went on countless interviews. Nothing seemed to fit. She continued to search the major job boards, e-mailed résumés, and kept her fingers crossed.

Job Seeker's Stumble

Mary did not have a well-thought-out career plan. She was not in charge of her job search; it was in charge of her. Without a clear career target in mind, up-to-date knowledge of career exploration tools, and effective job search methods, Mary was floundering. She was in a cycle of aimlessly sending résumés, taking whatever was offered out of desperation, and ending up frustrated in one dead-end job after another.

Job Seeker's ⋛New Strategy⋚

Being in charge of your career requires persistence and hard work, certainly characteristics Mary exhibited. However, there were some key factors missing that would have elevated Mary's career from ho-hum to wholly fulfilling. Specifically:

▷ **Self-Knowledge:** Awareness of the unique abilities, strengths, talents, and experience that could be used as benchmarks for finding the right career fit.

▷ **Career Exploration and Insight:** Use of career-discovery tools such as career assessments, career counseling/coaching, and informational interviews to find out about different companies and careers that would have been more satisfying on both personal and practical levels.

▷ **Personal Branding:** The unique value proposition you can bring to a potential employer, based on your authenticity that differentiates you from other candidates.

▷ **Effective Job Search Methods:** More productive job-search strategies, such as networking (both in-person and online social networking) and direct contact with companies and their employees. Internet job search, reserved to major job boards, does not produce high-yield results, especially as you advance beyond being an entry-level candidate.

▷ **Courage:** Getting out of your "comfort zone" and trying new job search approaches based on lifelong career management takes personal resiliency and self-confidence. Often that self-confidence comes from knowing exactly what you uniquely have to offer, and why it is of such important value to a potential employer.

Mary got out of her comfort zone and hired a career coach. Together they developed Mary's personal-branding portfolio, which included a series of strengths stories (stories that showcase relevant strengths using the C-A-R [Challenge-Action-Results] format), a one-page biography, and her unique value statement. After developing her brand portfolio, her coach was able to partner with Mary to create a résumé that was focused on Mary's major work contributions, as well as her education and professional development experiences. The résumé included the position title she was aiming for, her value statement, and keywords to fit the position and highlight her accomplishments. Finally, they developed a focused job search strategy with a step-by-step plan of action and did some role-playing to ease Mary's transition into a proactive and strategic job seeker.

Mary got excited about networking and marketing her brand. Within a few days, she had five networking meetings and two informational interviews lined up. One of those informational interviews developed into the creation of a new job for Mary—as Music Programming and Marketing Director for a regional symphony orchestra. Mary traded in her dead-end job for the job of her dreams in just a couple of months!

Chart Your Career Future With Care
Job Seeker's Story
Sarah had pursued a career in social work for 12 years starting right out of college with her bachelor's degree in social work. She was well-liked by her clients, co-workers, and supervisors, and consequently had gotten promoted to a managerial role. Initially she was excited about her promotion, but over time she found she dreaded going to work.

In Sarah's off-hours she was actively involved as a volunteer in the local animal shelter and a rescue-dog training program. In fact, she found more and more of her time at work was spent thinking about her volunteer jobs. When her friends asked her why she gave so much of her energy and time to these causes, Sarah had to admit that her heart was with her animal friends.

As Sarah continued volunteering over the years she was asked to speak to groups for fund-raising purposes about the animal shelter and rescue-dog training program. Because she was so passionate about these causes, it was easy for Sarah to convey her enthusiasm and clearly articulate the dire need both non-profits had for public support. In the four years that Sarah gave fund-raising presentations, more than $50,000 in private donations and company-matching funds had been received. Sarah never felt more alive than when she was talking about the programs to individuals and groups, educating them and trying to get them to help in some way.

One day Sarah had a lightbulb moment. She realized that the "job of her dreams" had more to do with what she did in her off-hours than what she did in her full-time job. But she didn't know what to do next. After all, her full-time job paid well and had decent benefits. She couldn't just give it up! The practical side of Sarah's nature won out. She settled into her full-time job with resignation, and began doing less and less for the animal shelter and rescue-dog training program. Sarah was de-motivated and stuck. She wondered, *"How could my life have turned out this way?"*

Job Seeker's Stumble

Sarah's newfound insight into a career field she could love got mired in a negative attitude, confused thinking, and limited horizons. Her first step in the direction of a career change was stopped in its tracks because Sarah had never learned how to manage her career, including the career change process. According to the Bureau of Labor Statistics, 10–14 job changes (which can include career changes) are the average for a working lifetime. With that in mind, wouldn't it have made sense for Sarah to proactively figure out her next career move and learn how to make career changes for the future? Instead, Sarah opted to remain passive about her career and her career choices. With self-imposed limited horizons, Sarah was doomed to be at the mercy of the winds of change that would surely affect her current job and career.

Job Seeker's ≥New Strategy≤

Even if you believe staying at your present job is the "smart" thing to do, regardless of how much you hate it, it is unlikely the job you have will stay there for you over the long term. In an increasingly fast-moving world of change, careers and industries come and go, or morph and evolve. By proactively meeting this challenge, your career future can likewise evolve and thrive. The following five-step career planning process can help you with career management for a lifetime:

1. **Assessment:** Explore and compile your complete portfolio of career assets, including your skills and strengths, interests and passions, personal brand, values and goals, personality type, education and training, work experience (paid and non-paid), and preferred work environment. These can be gathered through the use of in-depth formal career assessments and more informal, reflective career tools, such as thought-provoking "insight" questions and assignments, and feedback from others who know you well.

2. **Awareness:** Use what you find in the first step to deepen your understanding and awareness of what value you uniquely have to offer and what you really want from a career and a job. Think both long-term and short-term. Oftentimes, to reach the job of your dreams you need to create career bridges of interim jobs. Then, do some research on occupations, industries (1,170 are tracked by the Bureau of Labor Statistics), work sectors, and companies to find the best match with your assets. Employers look for candidates who are a "quality match" with their companies

and for the positions advertised. Shouldn't you be doing the same? You can research online by:

> Doing a Google search of Websites, groups, blogs, and news.

> Checking out Amazon.com for relevant books and videos.

> Using the resources of the public library or your local college's career center.

> Exploring online resources (see pages 165–166).

> Informational interviewing with individuals in different careers, industries, and work sectors of interest.

> Attending a professional association meeting or seminar, and networking for information and contacts.

> Volunteering or taking on an adult internship.

> Job shadowing (for example, at VocationVacations.com).

3. **Attitude:** In addition to clear thinking and awareness about your assets and value, proactive career management for a lifetime requires a positive attitude, willingness to take a well-calculated risk, and personal courage. It also means learning from your mistakes and looking for the opportunities that abound everywhere, even within your mistakes. Without this proactive attitude, insight into yourself and career research will lie fallow and die. Work on your attitude so your dreams for a better job and career have fertile ground in which to flourish.

4. **Actions:** Take the newfound knowledge about your career assets and "quality matched" options in the world of work (which includes self-employment), and make a critical commitment to yourself to ACT! Despite your fear and apprehension, narrow down your choices to something you can pursue now. Strategize long-term goals based on values,

needs, passions, purpose, and life/balance concerns. Then plot out a specific action plan aligned with your personal brand to get you there, perhaps in one big leap or in small "bridging" steps. Eliminate obstacles and problems and create the kind of conditions you need to make your branded action plan achievable. Chunk down the big goals into small ones, and tie everything to measurable time frames. These actions will transform your insights into the reality of a career and/or job you can love.

5. **Attraction:** Remembering that your next career move will likely not be your last, vow to update and re-assess your personal brand and career growth, network continually, practice lifelong learning to optimize your assets, and keep track of your accomplishments. Staying committed to and in control of your own career development and personal-branding identity will allow you to attract the people and opportunities that are right for your career future every step of the way.

Working with a well-qualified career counselor or career coach can help move the five-step process along and provide structure, guidance, and accountability. In addition, the following resources and links are useful for career exploration and self-discovery:

Employability Check-up	*www.acinet.org/acinet/ employabilitycheckup/emp_ask.asp*
Career Focus Quiz	*www.assessmentgoddess.com/ careerfocusquiz.html*
O'NET Career Exploration Tools	*www.onetcenter.org/tools.html*
Reach Branding Club	*www.reachbrandingclub.com*
Online Identity Calculator	*www.careerdistinction.com/onlineid/*
Best Careers 2008 (*U.S. News & World Report*)	*www.usnews.com/features/business/ best-careers/best-careers-2008.html*

CareerOneStop—Explore Careers	*www.careeronestop.org/Explore Careers/ExploreCareers.aspx*
Bureau of Labor Statistics	*www.bls.gov*
America's Career InfoNet	*www.acinet.org/acinet/*
Gateway to Associations	*www.asaecenter.org/Directories/ AssociationSearch.cfm? navItemNumber=16581*
Skills Profiler	*www.careerinfonet.org/Skills/*
Occupational Outlook Handbook	*www.bls.gov/oco/home.htm*
O'NET Online	*online.onetcenter.org/*
Occupational Outlook Quarterly	*www.bls.gov/opub/ooq/ooqindex.html*
Career Voyages	*www.careervoyages.gov/*
Crosswalk Search (military to civilian, apprenticeship training to occupations)	*online.onetcenter.org/crosswalk/*
DisabilityInfo	*www.disabilityinfo.gov/digov-public/ public/DisplayPage.do? parentFolderId=500*
Local Employment Dynamics	*lehd.did.census.gov/led/datatools/ datatools.html*
Vault.com	*www.vault.com*
Wetfeet.com	*www.wetfeet.com*
College Search on CollegeNET	*cnsearch.collegenet.com/cgi-bin/CN/ index*
Richard Bolles's *What Color Is Your Parachute?*	*www.jobhuntersbible.com*
Quintessential Careers	*www.quintcareers.com*
Career Guide to Industries	*www.bls.gov/oco/cg*
Match a Major to Job Listings	*6steps.monster.com/step1/ careerconverter/*
Idealist Guide to Non-Profit Careers	*www.idealist.org/careerguide*
Federal Jobs by Major	*www.usajobs.opm.gov/ei23.asp*

Lack of Research Fatal to Career Progress

Job Seeker's Story

Tom, an experienced Mechanical Engineer in the Michigan automotive industry, was at his wit's end. After having gained and lost or left nine jobs within 11 years, he was stymied in his job search. His track record of jobs appeared to be job hopping, but Tom knew there were good reasons why each job had ended, such as company mergers and bankruptcies, lay-offs, and even one job he had to leave after just six months (insurance salesman). The problem was that Tom wasn't being given a chance to explain these "good reasons" to employers and recruiters, and he was baffled about how to make his case.

After one year of an unsuccessful job search, Tom retained a career coach to help him with his résumé. Tom felt sure that if his résumé were somehow "fixed," he would have no problem getting interviews.

When Tom explained his job history to the coach, she asked, *"How did you find each of your jobs?"* In every case, Tom said it was an Internet job posting.

The coach went on to ask, *"How much research did you do about the company prior to the interview?"* Uncomfortable seconds passed while Tom fidgeted and then unhappily admitted he had done no research at all! Because he was desperate to find a job with a steady income and benefits, he felt he had to take every job offer. Looking back, Tom realized that strategy had backfired.

Many of the companies Tom had joined had been in dire straits financially or on the verge of being bought out. It was only a matter of a few months before Tom was on the streets again as a job seeker. The longest stint of his employment at any one company was nine months!

Job Seeker's Stumble

Tom's desperation coupled with his lack of company and industry research consistently landed his career in hot water.

Even when Tom tried a career change, he ended up in a field so unsuited to him that he felt compelled to leave. Tom needed more from his career coach than just a strategy for presenting his résumé; he first needed coaching on the importance of and methods for company and industry research as absolutely essential components of an effective job search for long-term success.

Job Seeker's ≷New Strategy≶

Tom's lack of research into industry trends and companies' backgrounds, including their financial and business status, proved fatal to his career progression. Whereas Tom failed to research companies, employment reviewers and recruiters customarily research candidates to determine who to bring in for interviews, and, after more in-depth research, who will get job offers. According to a 2007 survey by ExecuNet, 83 percent of recruiters use search engines to learn about candidates; furthermore, 43.4 percent of recruiters who use the Internet to check out prospects say they have eliminated candidates based on what they found online. Wouldn't it have made sense for Tom to have also used the same selective-research rationale to determine which companies were best bets for interviewing and which ones he could pass up?

Stay organized in your search by drilling down tier by tier: industries, companies, key players, and jobs. Tom could have started with industry research to gain a "big-picture" perspective into the automotive industry, as well as the medical-device industry where he felt he might have a better future. This kind of research yields overall trend information that could have helped Tom as he planned and managed his career future.

Then Tom could have proactively researched top companies in those industries to approach, as well as researching companies that appeared in job postings of interest. That would have maximized his job search efforts by allowing him to eliminate companies with questionable histories or that appeared to be financially distressed.

Finally, within each of the companies that survived his selective-research process, Tom could have researched the appropriate department heads (key players) to contact, as well as researching specific interviewers by name. Asking questions and connecting with other professionals on social networking Websites such as LinkedIn, Ryze, and Facebook could also have yielded "insider" information on industry trends, company culture and values, referrals to key players, and job openings. Armed with this kind of information, Tom would have quickly become recognized as a high-quality and sought-after candidate.

This tiered research method does take some time, but can be done easily using online and offline resources. The following list represents a sampling of the resources Tom could have used, grouped by categories:

Industries and Professional Occupations

American Society for Quality	*www.asq.org*
American Society of Mechanical Engineers (ASME)	*www.asme.org*
Bureau of Labor Statistics (industry)	*www.bls.gov*
Encyclopedia of Associations (library reference)	*library.dialog.com/bluesheets/ html/bl0114.html*
Gateway to Associations	*www.asaecenter.org/Directories/ AssociationSearch.cfm? navItemNumber=16581*
Mechanical Engineering Magazine	*www.memagazine.org/*
Medical Devicelink	*www.devicelink.com/*
National Society for Professional Engineers	*www.nspe.org*
Occupational Outlook Quarterly (industry)	*www.bls.gov/opub/ooq/ ooqindex.html*
Regional Economic Conditions (RECON)	*www2.fdic.gov/recon/*
Society of Automotive Engineers	*www.sae.org*

Company Financials

BigCharts	*www.bigcharts.com*
CNN Money	*money.cnn.com/*
Corporate Directory of U.S. Public Companies (library reference)	*www.researchandmarkets.com/ reports/302094*
	www.amazon.com/Corporate-Directory-Us-Public-Companies/ dp/B00006KA9P
Edgar Online	*www.edgar-online.com*
Google Finance	*finance.google.com*
MarketWatch	*www.marketwatch.com*
MSN Money	*moneycentral.msn.com*
NASDAQ Trader	*www.nasdaqtrader.com*
SEC Info	*www.secinfo.com*
Yahoo! Finance	*finance.yahoo.com*

Industries/Companies/Key Players

About.com	*www.about.com*
Advanced Google Search	*www.google.com/advanced_search*
Alta Vista	*www.altavista.com*
America's Career InfoNet Employer Finder	*www.acinet.org/acinet/ employerlocator/ employerlocator.asp*
Business.com	*www.business.com*
Business Journal	*www.bizjournals.com*
Business Wire	*www.businesswire.com*
Career Journal	*www.careerjournal.com*
CEOExpress	*www.ceoexpress.com*
Clusty	*clusty.com*
Corporate Information	*www.corporateinformation.com*
Fast Company	*www.fastcompany.com*
Fortune 500	*money.cnn.com/magazines/fortune/ fortune500/*

Industries/Companies/Key Players (continued)

Fortune Magazine	*www.fortune.com*
Global 500	*money.cnn.com/magazines/ fortune/global500/2006/*
Google Blog Search	*blogsearch.google.com*
Hoovers	*www.hoovers.com*
Inc. 500	*www.inc.com/inc5000/ index.html*
Internet Public Library	*www.ipl.org*
Job-Hunt	*www.job-hunt.org*
List of Lists	*www.specialissues.com/lol/*
MagPortal	*www.magportal.com*
Michigan Newspapers	*www.newslink.org/minews.html*
Private 500	*www.forbes.com/fdc/ welcome_mjx.shtml*
Reuters	*www.reuters.com*
Technorati (blog search)	*www.technorati.com*
Thomas Net	*www.thomasnet.com/index.html*
Topix	*www.topix.com*
Vault.com	*www.vault.com*
WetFeet.com	*www.wetfeet.com*

Social Networking

Corporate Alumni	*www.corporatealumni.com*
Ecademy	*www.ecademy.com*
Facebook	*www.facebook.com*
LinkedIn.com	*www.linkedin.com*
MySpace	*www.myspace.com*
Plaxo	*www.plaxo.com*
Ryze	*www.ryze.com*
Tribe	*www.tribe.com*
Zoominfo	*www.zoominfo.com*

Jobs Boards/Search Engines

AIRS Directory (jobs)	*www.airsdirectory.com*
AssociationJobBoards.com	*www.associationjobboards.com*
CareerOneStop	*careeronestop.org*
CareerXRoads	*www.careerxroads.com*
Craigslist	*www.craigslist.com*
EmploymentGuide.com	*www.employmentguide.com*
Engineer.net	*www.engineer.net*
Experience	*www.experience.com*
JobsInManufacturing.com	*www.jobsinmanufacturing.com*
Kennedy Guide to Executive Recruiters (library reference; fee)	*www.recruiterredbook.com/ index.php*
Local Careers	*www.localcareers.com*
MechanicalEngineer.com	*www.mechanicalengineer.com*
Mega Job Search Engines	*www.indeed.com www.simplyhired.com*
Michigan Talent Bank	*www.michworks.org*
NicheBoards.com	*www.nicheboards.com*
Recruiters Online Network	*recruitersonline.com*
USAJobs	*www.usajobs.gov*
Yahoo! HotJobs (jobs)	*www.hotjobs.com*

No Proof of Value Means No Job Offer

Job Seeker's Story

Derrick had steeled himself for an intense job search after being laid off. With a 13-year background in Robotics Engineering in the automotive industry, Derrick knew he would have a difficult time finding new employment in a tight economy.

Prepared to move anywhere for a job in his field, Derrick had responded to online job postings for Robotics Engineering positions nationwide. He needed an income immediately, so he decided that replying to many job postings would maximize the number of interviews he could expect. After four months with no responses, Derrick decided to consult with a professional résumé writer.

When the résumé writer reviewed Derrick's résumé, it looked as though he had used his job description to fashion the bullet points on his résumé, which included entries such as:

- Serviced and maintained paint production line.
- Implemented quality procedures.
- Troubleshot production-paint anomalies.
- Communicated with customers to resolve complaints.

Derrick was surprised to learn that employers needed more information than what he had provided on his résumé. *"After all,"* he thought, *"my references will attest to what a great worker I am."* The problem is that Derrick was not getting to the stage in the application process where references would be contacted. Consequently, he was not getting interviews or job offers.

Job Seeker's Stumble

By using a standard job description to characterize his potential value to a company, Derrick had relegated himself to the status of one among many other Robotics Engineers with similar job descriptions. Without any proof of accomplishments or value, why would any employer be interested in having a conversation with Derrick, when any Robotics Engineer would do? Over the years, Derrick had done a good job, worked diligently, and had a positive impact on his past company's bottom-line financial performance. Now he needed to prove that in his résumé so prospective employers would take notice of him and extend an offer for an interview.

Job Seeker's New Strategy

Although Derrick made it past the employment reviewer's first hurdle of credibility (Derrick had indeed worked in

Robotics Engineering for 13 years), he did not make it past the hurdle of value. Value is a key criterion in the employment reviewer's decision-making process as he or she scans an applicant's résumé. It certainly plays a pivotal role in deciding who to interview and, ultimately, who to hire.

To strengthen Derrick's résumé and demonstrate value to the potential employer, the following changes were made in his bulleted points. Specifically:

- **Troubleshooting:** Improved resolution of paint-defect rate up to 99% and saved $12,000 annually by proactively monitoring and troubleshooting six production lines.

- **Quality Control Leadership:** Played key role in quality-control certification for just-in-time (JIT) manufacturing plant by establishing and managing QS9000 policies and procedures.

- **Process Improvements:** Secured $4.8 million in annual cost savings through manufacturing process innovation and improvements which lowered scrap yields and decreased downtime by 160 hours per year.

- **New Business Development:** Won $1.2 million in new business contracts over two years by outstripping competitors' turnaround time for color-matching process. Collaborated with clients' color teams to resolve complaints and institute new technologies to fine-tune color matches.

With these valuable accomplishments on his résumé, Derrick found that his success rate in landing interviews increased significantly. He also realized that by isolating and quantifying his specific accomplishments, he had regained a large measure of self-esteem he had lost when he was laid off. More importantly, Derrick could now talk convincingly in an interview about his value and answer the question, *"Why should I hire you?"* with cost-saving and revenue-generating results. When the return on investment for the employer to hire a particular candidate becomes apparent and compelling, it then becomes easy to make the hiring decision.

Personal Branding to Stand Out From the Crowd

Job Seeker's Story

Josh was astonished when he was let go after his company in the medical electronics instrumentation industry was bought out by its top competitor. Because Josh had been number one in sales for the past five years (out of his six years with the company), he assumed he was vital to company operations and, thus, immune from company layoffs.

Because he never imagined he would be job-hunting anytime soon, Josh did not have an up-to-date résumé ready to go. While he struggled with writing one, he started getting "nibbles" of interest from other companies in the industry, as well as related industries. Hoping to capitalize on their interest, Josh hurriedly crafted a reverse-chronological listing of jobs he had held with snippets of job descriptions for each. He even included a couple of accomplishments, including his number-one sales status. After e-mailing his one-page résumé, Josh sat back and waited for what he was sure would be a flood of interview requests. Curiously, no interviews materialized.

Kevin found himself in a similar job search situation with no interviews. While Kevin was still employed at what he termed a "dead-end job" in the financial information-management industry, he had responded to online job postings with his updated résumé and gotten no interview offers. As a project manager, Kevin assumed his type of job would be in demand and, therefore, had spent little time on preparing his résumé. Kevin did include descriptions of five of his major projects in the past four years, and their ultimate outcomes. (In some cases the projects had died due to change of executive leadership and company priorities.)

Job Seeker's Stumble

Both Josh and Kevin started their résumés with their name and contact information, and then proceeded directly into listing their job history (with sparse descriptions and accomplishments) in reverse order, as well as education and training. Although Josh's and Kevin's résumés were an accurate depiction of their career histories, and did include minimal accomplishments, they did not persuade potential employment reviewers to contact them. In particular, the dry facts of their work history and educational background did nothing to convey their personality. For occupations in Sales and Project Management—where interpersonal, communications, and leadership skills are paramount—Josh and Kevin did not contribute any sense of their personal style, value-added benefits to the employer, and potential cultural fit.

Job Seeker's ≥New Strategy≥

Because companies typically invest thousands of dollars per hire in the recruiting and interviewing process, they do not seek out "ordinary" candidates who portray themselves on a résumé with deadly boring details or with no personality and impact. The reason extraordinary candidates stand out and get hired is that (1) they demonstrate value (benefits) that the employer absolutely wants, and (2) they showcase a memorable and positive personal brand that is a quality match between the candidate and the company/team.

For best self-marketing results, your message of value (what you can do of benefit to the employer) and your personal brand (how you do what you do) need to be consistent with your authentic self and made crystal clear to the employer. On a résumé, value and personal branding can be woven into every major element. For example, both Josh and Kevin could have started their résumés (after their contact information) with a Header, Tagline, and Summary that provided an overview of their value, brand, career history and accomplishments, and training. That would have meant even a cursory initial reading could have intrigued the employment reviewer enough to want to read more of the body of the résumé. Josh's Header and Tagline could have read:

Account Executive—Medical Electronics Instrumentation Products

Sales excellence through pain-free product education

Kevin's Header and Tagline might have been stated as:

Project Manager—Information Technology

Collaboration building for flawless projects—on time, every time

These Headers and Taglines demonstrate much-needed benefits to the employer (*"sales excellence"* and *"flawless projects"*) while also highlighting the way in which Josh and Kevin attained their stellar results (*"pain-free product education"* and *"collaboration building"*).

These themes could have been repeated throughout their résumés to reinforce their personal branding and to differentiate them from other candidates. By selectively describing the actions they took to achieve their accomplishments, for example, they could have shown the constancy of their brands. Josh could have mentioned his track record of upselling and cross-selling products (95 percent of every customer-service call and product demo) because of his unique skills in isolating customers' needs, addressing those needs in the "product-education" process, and making the technical information easy to understand.

Even education and volunteer involvement could serve to convey a common thread of personal branding. In Kevin's case, for example, his leadership as a Boy Scout Troop leader in fundraising projects could have been cited. His collaboration with the local chamber of commerce and community-service organizations proved essential to record-breaking fund-raisers.

What is your theme of uniqueness and differentiation? You have a personal brand, whether you know it or not, and that brand promises delivery of value to a potential employer. Once you are in touch with your personal brand and the value your brand produces, you can use those concepts in your self-marketing documents to ensure you will be the applicant asked in to interview. What's more, by selecting you to interview, the employer will have already pre-qualified you in terms of company-culture fit. Though it is true that employers need to know you can produce the results they need, they also must know that you will fit into the existing team dynamics and company.

To discover your brand, get honest feedback from others (friends, business colleagues, co-workers, supervisors, vendors and suppliers, customers, and so forth), or take the 360Reach Personal Branding Assessment (*www.reachcc.com/360register*). Look for consistent themes of personal style, strengths, and value you deliver. The following additional resources relate to personal branding discovery and branding communications:

Personal Branding Quiz	*www.assessmentgoddess.com/ brandingquiz.html*
The Brand Called You	*www.fastcompany.com/magazine/10/ brandyou.html*
Reach Branding Club	*www.reachbrandingclub.com*
Brand You World! Personal Branding Summit	*www.personalbrandingsummit.com*
Reach Communications	*www.reachcc.com*
Online Identity Calculator	*www.careerdistinction.com/onlineid/*

People have brands just as products and companies do. Your brand is your unique combination of skills, strengths, knowledge, and personal style that adds value to others. Rather than appearing just the same as every other job applicant, distinguish your résumé and cover letter with your personal branding message. Showcase your brand as "giving," positive, and uplifting, and others will be interested in you. It is through that interest that you will gain attention from employers who will be the best "quality match" for you.

CHAPTER 8

Interviewing Inadequacies

︿

Avoid a Sticky First Impression

Job Seeker's Story

Melvin McCreary loved to help people and had a degree in social work, so when he saw the job advertisement for a Weight-Loss Consultant, he thought this was a position in which he could be very successful. In fact, he had a personal interest in weight maintenance and wanted to help all those people who struggled with their weight. Melvin sent in his résumé and was successful in landing an interview.

When the date of his interview arrived, Melvin arrived 30 minutes early with a dozen doughnuts. Carrying in the box, he introduced himself jovially and told the receptionist that he thought it would make a lasting impression on his interviewer. Silently, the receptionist agreed; it was the first time she had seen doughnuts in the facility!

When Melvin met his interviewer, Sheena, he presented her with the doughnuts, stating, *"I knew it was early so I wanted to make sure you could get your breakfast."* She took the box and set it on her desk, not bothering to offer him one. Throughout the interview the box of doughnuts sat untouched and Melvin began to have doubts about bringing them.

At the end of the interview, Melvin said, *"I know dough-nuts are not very dietetic; I thought it would make a nice treat. I am sorry if I insulted you in some way."* Sheena looked at him for a few moments and said, *"Not at all. Thank you Melvin."*

Melvin left, not sure how to judge his interview with Sheena. He felt rather sheepish about having brought doughnuts and assumed he had made a bad choice.

Job Seeker's Stumble

Bringing a fattening snack food such as doughnuts to a weight-loss clinic, when you are interviewing for a position as a Weight-Loss Consultant, just lacks common sense. Melvin failed to get a job offer because he demonstrated to the inter-viewer that he had little understanding of what constituted healthy eating and seemed to lack sensitivity to the struggles of those who had weight problems. Thinking a sweet treat (in this case, a dozen doughnuts) was appropriate for a face-to-face interview left Melvin out of a job opportunity.

Job Seeker's ≳New Strategy≲

It is never a good idea to bring food to an interview, be-cause it simply opens up too many possibilities to make a bad impression. You do not know if the interviewer is a diabetic, has food allergies, or just will think you are a messy eater! Instead, view the interview as a professional meeting where you need to make a positive impression. Food does not come into that equation.

If you still want to bring something to the interview, think about what will enhance your opportunity for the particular job. For instance:

▷ As a Weight-Loss Consultant you might put together sample meal plans that demonstrate your knowledge of healthy, balanced eating. You might also bring motivational mate-rials or a counseling plan you have used in former social worker roles to show the interviewer.

▷ As a Sales Professional, you might have a brag book showing sales awards, charts that demonstrate quota attainment, follow-up tools and materials used with clients, or other benchmarks of performance.

▷ As an Artist, you might bring a portfolio of samples of work.

▷ As an Engineer, you might have a mock-up of a project or other physical examples of your work on CD, DVD, scale model, or in another visual media.

It is easy to make an interview more visual and more tangible without tangling with inappropriate (and frequently messy) food. Remember to always focus on professionalism and the type of position you are targeting.

Keep Negative Comments to Yourself

Job Seeker's Story

Stacey's job search had gone on for more than six months with no job offers, and she was getting discouraged. With 10 years of experience in Marketing and Marketing Management, plus a recent MBA in Marketing, Stacey had been with a company that had gone through re-structuring and drastic employee cuts after a merger. Stacey had decided on her own to leave and had no trouble in quickly landing interviews. But somehow they did not progress to the job-offer stage. As Stacey was pondering her situation, she received a phone call from Lenore, Human Resources Executive Director of a staffing firm, who indicated she would like to interview Stacey over the phone briefly for a Director of Marketing position. Stacey happily agreed.

Stacey and Lenore proceeded to have a very friendly conversation about Stacey's qualifications and past accomplishments. Lenore was impressed and already had mentally earmarked Stacey for an in-person interview when she asked her last question: "*Stacey, why did you leave your last marketing position?*"

Stacey took a deep breath and quickly responded, "*I left because my boss was a jerk. This guy had an ego the size of the*

Grand Canyon, and I just decided one day I had had enough. I would not put up with his overbearing attitude any longer. Within two weeks, I was out of there!"

Lenore gripped the phone, and, smiling tightly, replied, *"I see. Well, I think I have enough information. Thank you for your time."* Lenore had decided then and there to exclude Stacey from further consideration and crossed her name off the list of qualified applicants.

Maggie, another job seeker, met a similar fate in her face-to-face interview with Craig, the Vice President of Employment for a large financial-services firm. Maggie, a Recruiting Specialist, had also experienced a lengthy job search that included many interviews, but no job offers. As Craig asked the standard interviewing questions, he was forming a positive impression about Maggie and was seriously considering hiring her for the open recruiting position. Then Craig asked, *"If I were to speak to your current boss, what would he say about you?"*

Without skipping a beat, Maggie looked Craig in the eyes and replied, *"Well, we used to be friends. Then he did some things I didn't agree with. So I sued the clown and the company, and they lost. He probably wouldn't have anything favorable to say."*

Taken aback, Craig finished the interview, and, as he escorted Maggie out the door, wondered who the "lucky" employer would be to get Maggie next. It certainly would not be his company!

Job Seeker's Stumble

Both Stacey and Maggie committed the fatal *faux pas* of bad-mouthing a former employer, and, in Maggie's case, bragging about winning a lawsuit against her former company and boss! These harsh and ill-advised comments revealed their lack of good common sense, and insensitivity to an employer's concern about hiring egocentric (non-team-oriented) and litigious applicants who apparently lacked interpersonal, communications, and conflict-resolution skills.

Job Seeker's ⋛New Strategy⋚

Calling anyone, especially a previous boss, a "jerk" or a "clown" in an interview raises concerns about an applicant's professionalism and judgment. Keeping to the facts of the situation regarding any question is usually "safe" territory. The moment you interject a value judgment about a situation or another person—your boss, co-worker, client, consultant, supplier/vendor, or professional colleague, for example—you are treading on dangerous territory.

Likewise, revealing past actions that had a negative impact on a former employer is not exactly in the category of making a good impression. Your track record of behaviors, both good and bad, is seen as a predictor of future behavior. Do you think any employer would welcome an applicant with a track record of suing his or her employer? The element of risk involved would likely be seen as outweighing the benefits from hiring such a person.

Both of the examples here could have been handled more diplomatically by the interviewees. Specifically:

▷ **Re-assess the Facts:** If Stacey had looked at the situation again, she could have extracted the facts and used them to explain her departure. For example, in response to Lenore's final question, Stacey could have said, "*Having seen the 'writing on the wall' with employees being downsized in every department after the company's merger and re-structuring, I realized I needed to begin a full-time job search immediately. To accommodate that planning, I did give two-weeks' notice and put in full-time hours until I left.*"

▷ **Re-frame the Situation:** Rather than highlighting the conflict in a situation, draw out the positives and what you learned; then look for common ground for agreement with the interviewer. For example, Maggie could have said, "*I believe my former employer would agree that I learned a lot in my last recruiting position that has made me a well-rounded*

recruiter, especially in online talent sourcing and group pre-
sentations to potential candidates. One of the major les-
sons I learned had to do with ethical recruiting practices. I
place high importance on ethics and transparency in re-
cruiting. What is your view on ethics and recruiting?" By
taking this stance, Maggie would have positioned herself
as taking the "high ground" and probed for agreement.
Thus, even if the VP discovered the successful lawsuit
against her former employer, it could be interpreted against
the background of her positively stated explanation.

The bottom line is to keep any bad-mouthing and name-
calling out of the interview, no matter how much you disliked
your last boss, company, or co-worker. Harsh and negative
personal judgments can only make you look bad. Likewise, re-
framing a negative situation to extract learning points can impress an employment reviewer with your tact, professionalism,
and positive attitude.

When Honesty Is Overboard

Job Seeker's Story

Nancy had injured herself on a job and endured back surgery and painful rehabilitation. Determined to never again en-
danger her back, she heeded her doctor's warning to never do
any heavy lifting and made sure prospective employers knew
about her restrictions in the first interview, even though her career field was Receptionist and did not require any heavy lifting.

Larry had bad knees and had undergone surgery on his left
knee. He was advised by his physician that he may, someday,
require surgery on his other knee. He was applying for a position as Manager in a large insurance agency, a position that
would not put stress on his knees. Yet, on every interview, he
told prospective employers that he was anticipating having knee
surgery in the future that would put him out of work for three
to four months.

Bill had a long history of alcoholism when he finally accepted help and went into rehabilitation. He had been sober for 18 months and was so proud of his accomplishment that he shared his success with all prospective employers, believing his strength of will and personal commitment to sobriety spoke volumes about his integrity and work ethic.

Nancy, Larry, and Bill each suffered the same outcome: They did not hear back from the employers with whom they met. They felt frustrated and hurt that these employers did not respect their honesty and integrity.

Job Seeker's Stumble

Yes, each of these job seekers should be praised for their honesty. However, in each case they disclosed information about themselves that was not asked of them, was not relevant to their ability to perform the requirements of the job, and provided the employer with a potential negative concern: higher insurance expenses, extended time out of work, and the potential for a relapse, which would affect job performance and attendance, respectively.

Job Seeker's ≥New Strategy≤

If you have any type of a health limitation, it is important to seek out and apply only for positions that you can do successfully and that do not require you to further injure yourself. In these cases, your disabilities or injuries do not impact on your ability to perform the job and are therefore not relevant. You might think that both Larry and Bill need to disclose, but Larry does not have a set commitment or schedule for surgery, or even the certainty that he will need the surgery in the next year, so he should not bring it to the forefront in a first interview. If Bill continues his sobriety, his alcoholism is also not relevant. Because he can only take it one day at a time and assume he will stay sober, it will not have bearing on his ability to perform the job.

So, do not assume the worst and feel that you have to disclose everything in a first interview! Should you learn in the interview that there are elements of the job that would be a problem (such as unexpected heavy lifting for a Receptionist position), you should wait to discuss these concerns once there is an offer on the table. Then and only then will you be in a position of being the one they know they want to hire and might make a concession to do so. However, if it is just not relevant to the job, such as the sobriety or the potential of a surgery this year or five years later, you should keep it to yourself, because it will not affect the job you will perform today.

Asking Questions Shows Your Interest

Job Seeker's Story

Parrish consulted a career coach because he had been to more than 100 interviews and never received a second interview or an offer. In the practice sessions, his coach quickly discovered that, when asked if he had any questions near the end of the interview, Parrish would always politely respond that he did not.

When the coach asked Parrish why he never asked questions, he responded, *"I'm there to be interviewed by them, right?"*

Job Seeker's Stumble

Parrish made a fundamental mistake in his interviews by not asking any questions. Employers leave space at the end of an interview with an expectation that a candidate has questions. This segment of the interview is so important that, in some cases, employers may overlook other interview mistakes such as arriving late or poor appearance if you demonstrate your motivation through a few well-defined questions.

Job Seeker's ≷New Strategy≷

Asking questions is critical to the interview, but you must also ask the *right* questions. An interviewer wants to know you are engaged with the job opportunity. Asking the right questions shows you did your research, and that is a major factor in determining whether an employer would hire you or not. The following areas are good starting points for questions:

> Key company goals for the coming year.

> How the team operates and general cultural norms.

> What challenges the department is facing.

Some examples of good questions include:

▷ What are the top three priorities you want to see accomplished this quarter?

▷ How long has this team worked together, and what can I offer to enhance it?

▷ What do you feel is the most successful profile for this position?

▷ I noticed on the Website that the company is moving into a new market sector. How does this position affect that?

▷ What traits and attributes are you seeking in the right candidate for this position?

Make sure that you structure questions as open-ended and relevant, because you always want to tie your value proposition back to the company's success. Never make the interviewer feel uncomfortable by asking questions that are too complex, seem to request proprietary information, or are silly (such as asking if the company offers free food or beverages). Use caution when asking questions regarding your fit to a position. Asking too many questions about your match to the needs of the position may seem to be a hard sell to an interviewer. Also, hold off on compensation questions. Remember that questions about salary and benefits will be discussed eventually if you make it to the short list of interested candidates.

Asking the right questions is a core skill for all job seekers to master. Make sure you come prepared so that you leave an impression and stand out from your competition.

Unprepared Is Unsuccessful

Job Seeker's Story

Paulina felt as if she was in the middle of a bad dream: She had slept through her alarm, got a speeding ticket when she raced to be on time to her interview, and now could not even remember which job she was interviewing for at Elvernon Corporation. Was this the Project Manager position with Steve Jones, or was it the PMO Director role with Terrence Miller? In her haste she had left the information at home.

It turned out she was meeting with Terrence about the PMO role, and all seemed to be progressing smoothly until he asked her what she knew about Elvernon. Paulina was speechless, as she thought that was one of the things she was there to learn from the interviewer. She said, *"I know that I want to work here and that I would do a great job for you."*

The interviewer was silent for an uncomfortable amount of time. Finally he resumed the interview as if nothing had happened. When Paulina left she thought she had recovered nicely, but she did not hear from Terrence or Elvernon again.

Job Seeker's Stumble

Paulina made the critical mistake of not preparing effectively before her interview. This preparation goes far beyond showing up on time; it relates to conducting research on the target company to understand their goals, their mission, their products, and even their challenges prior to the interview. By doing this, Paulina could have confidently woven her knowledge of the company into her interview.

Job Seeker's ⋛New Strategy⋜

When you are targeting a company in your search, it is important that you perform research so that you can demonstrate to the interviewer how you can meet the goals and needs of the organization. The type of information you will want includes:

> Company goals and mission.

> Products and/or services offered.

> Recent changes in the organization, such as emerging technology, new products, expansions, mergers, and so forth.

> Company history.

Also, for your own information, it is a good idea to check financials on the company to ensure its worthiness or buoyancy.

By researching these areas, you can gain a knowledgeable edge on positioning yourself during the interview. As a matter of fact, this extra work will increase your confidence and will keep you from walking blind into your interview. Some of the ways you might find this information include:

Small/Local Companies

The smaller the company, the less information may be available about them to the public. Try these sources:

▷ **Yellow Pages:** The first thing you should do is look in your telephone yellow pages. For instance, if you have an interview with Joe's Plumbing for an Office Manager position, you would first check to see if the company has an ad in the book. If it does, you can probably find out some valuable information about it. In this case, Joe's Plumbing has been in business for 23 years, is a member of the Better Business Bureau, and offers several services. Joe's ad does not list a Web address, but another company's ad might display one, so you should always be sure to look for one.

▷ **Buddy System:** Get other people involved in supporting your information gathering by forming a team with another job seeker, husband, girlfriend, sister, and so forth, and then having him or her do some research for you. You certainly do not want to walk into the lobby of the company you are scheduled to interview with, or call and have your voice recognized. Your buddy will not be stressed because she has nothing at stake in doing your research. Ask her to call the company and ask a few questions. The easiest way is for her to pose as a potential customer and ask for information. For instance, with a doctor's office, she might say, *"I'm looking for a specialist for my mother. Can you tell me a little about the doctor's credentials? How long has he been practicing?"*

The walk-in option works best with retail or customer-oriented organizations. You might send your buddy in to gather up any brochures or documentation on the company. If your buddy is brave, she might even be coaxed into asking questions as if she were job searching in order to learn more about the company.

▷ **Local Business Organizations:** Try contacting the chamber of commerce, local Better Business Bureau, newspaper information desk, or any local business publications. If a company is a member of the chamber or one of the local papers has written an article on the company, you should be able to gain information easily.

Large Companies/Corporations

With larger companies, the resources are virtually endless. Try these:

▷ **Company Website:** The single best resource is the company Website. Most companies post their annual report as well as all the information you could ever want to know about their goals, mission, services, products, officers, locations, and press online.

▷ **Annual Report:** No Website? Look for an annual report. Frequently going directly to the company for this can be somewhat sticky. You might try your local reference librarian for help in finding annual reports and online/newspaper articles on the company.

▷ **Library Resources:** The reference librarian can also direct you to a number of resources in the library, such as:

> *Corporate Technology Directory* by CorpTech.

> *Directory of Corporate Affiliations* by Reed Reference Publishing Company.

> *Directory of Leading Private Companies* by National Register Publishing Company.

> *Hospital Phone Book* by U.S. Directory Service.

> *International Directory of Corporate Affiliates* by National Register Publishing Company.

> *Sales Guide to High-Tech Companies* by CorpTech.

▷ **Internet Resources:** There are also excellent resources that can be accessed through the Internet, including:

> **Google Advanced Search** will let you scan news stories from the past week. *www.google.com/advanced_search*

> **Hoover's Online** provides timely and detailed information on more than 50,000 public and private companies. *www.hoovers.com*

> **News Directory** and **Newslink** allows you to browse trade publications and regional publications. *www.newsdirectory.com* and *www.newslink.org/mbiz.html*

> **Corporate Information** provides U.S. and international company information including research reports, company profiles, earnings information, and analyst reports. *www.corporateinformation.com*

> **Business.com** offers news, research, and contacts for 10,000 public companies and 44,000 private companies. *www.business.com*

> **Pacific Information Resources, Inc.** includes information on private companies in its public record databases. *www.pac-info.com*

> > **American Society of Association Executives** is a gateway of more than 6,589 associations that offers a comprehensive directory to Websites of business and professional associations. *www.asaecenter.org/Directories/AssociationSearch.cfm?navItemNumber=16581*

> > **Yahoo Finance Global Ticker Symbol Lookup** allows you to identify the ticker symbol for a public company. *quote.yahoo.com/lookup*

> **Networking:** You should also look at your network. Are you a member of a professional organization in this industry? Can you contact members who work within the company or peruse organization journals? Do you know someone who knows someone? Additionally, you should consider the wealth of online social networking resources now available on the Internet, such as LinkedIn and Facebook, to find someone who has the information you are seeking.

Once you have gathered all your information, read through and organize it. Highlight key information and questions the information generates, and then create a brief summary. Study this, and be prepared to integrate it into your interview.

By taking just a little time, you will be ready to enter your interview with knowledge and confidence. You will be positioned to succeed by making a positive impression.

Wanted: Professional Interview Behavior

Job Seeker's Story

Terrence was one of a soon-to-graduate class of MBA students from a top university. He had been invited to the first round of interviews with the senior leadership finance team of a Fortune 500 company. Terrence was excited about this interview because he had heard that the starting salary would be $90,000 with a $10,000 sign-on bonus and relocation expenses paid. As Terrence juggled his final semester classes and projects, he also prepared for the interview by researching the company. When he discovered that the company's MBA recruiting program was a new one, he felt lucky to be included in the first round of interviewees. In fact, he was to be the first interviewee in the schedule rotation.

He was very busy trying to "wrap up" his last semester activities, so Terrence did not get a chance to prepare for the interview as much as he would have liked. However, he thought the company research he had done could be put to good use in the interview. As Terrence answered the interviewing panel's questions, he tried to tie in his skills with the services the company offered. Terrence felt he was doing well when suddenly his pager beeped, and he asked to be excused to make a phone call. He explained he was working on an important project, and, because he was critical to the success of the project, he had to immediately respond. Terrence left to make the call from the hallway.

Ten minutes later Terrence returned to the conference room, where the interviewing panel had quietly been gathering up their paperwork in preparation to move on to the next candidate. They decided to resume the interview with Terrence and had gotten through two more questions when Terrence's pager beeped a second time. Again, Terrence asked to be excused, explaining how vital he was to the project. This time he was gone for five minutes. When Terrence returned the interviewers quickly completed the interview, shook his hand, and escorted him out of the conference room.

Immediately following the interview with Terrence the panel called their company's Human Resources Director. They explained that they had decided not to hire Terrence and why, relating the story of Terrence's unprofessional and disrespectful behavior. In fact, the interviewing panel was so disturbed by Terrence, they decided not to hire any student from that particular university's MBA program!

Job Seeker's Stumble

Terrence's lack of good manners and unprofessional behavior, combined with his egocentric "bragging" about his role on a team project, totally turned off a three-member management team tasked with recruiting new MBAs. Unfortunately, Terrence's behavior made such a bad first impression that it affected every other student on the interviewers' schedule negatively: None of them even got the chance to interview. In this case, the results of Terrence's actions had widespread effects, which he did not learn until after the interview.

Job Seeker's ≷New Strategy≷

Professionalism and good manners are critical in interviews, whether on the phone or in person, with an individual or in a group. Social conduct that is sensitive to and shows regard for others, rather than ignoring or downgrading others, is the central concept of exhibiting professionalism. In Terrence's case, his unprofessional behavior included the subtle message that he and his class projects were "more important" than the interviewers and their time. Review the following tips for guidelines on professional behavior in the interview:

▷ **Be on Time:** Show up at the appointed time, not excessively early and not late.

▷ **Stay for the Entire Interview:** Do not step out to make or take phone calls.

▷ **Turn Off Your Cell Phone/Pager:** Be fully present at the interview.

▷ **Dress Professionally and Be Clean:** Being unkempt, disheveled, dirty, or too informal (for example, rings in tongue, eyebrows, and so on) will make an impression, but not the one needed to get hired by the vast majority of employers.

▷ **Listen Carefully to the Questions Asked:** Do not attempt to multitask during an interview. You will need your full powers of concentration to evaluate the "question behind the question." For example, *"Why did it take you five years to complete your bachelor's degree program rather than the standard four?"* really means, *"We are fearful. Is something amiss in your academic or personal life?"*

▷ **Keep Your Ego in Check:** Although you do want to talk about your relevant accomplishments to the position for which you are being interviewed, be careful not to brag, exaggerate, or sound arrogant, especially if you were part of a team effort.

▷ **Hone Your Sensitivity:** Be aware of potential "land mines" in the verbal exchange that revolve around political, ethnic, gender, and religious issues. Research and understand the company culture, which the interviewer will likely represent, so you can respond to it appropriately.

▷ **Respect the Interviewer's Time:** Frame succinct and meaningful responses to questions. Avoid jargon and language that is too technical, unless you are interviewing with a technical person. Prepare Context-Challenge-Actions-Results (C-C-A-R) stories for key skills needed in the position and keep editing them for brevity and clarity. You can tell a story with impact in less than 60 seconds!

▷ **Respect the Interviewer:** Show respect first with good manners, and you will engender respect in return. An interview does not have to be a clash of wills or a cross-examination. Instead, it can be a fact-finding mission and persuasive conversation for both the interviewee and the interviewer.

▷ **Use Clear, Non-Confusing Language:** Tape-record your answers to typical interview questions in your practice sessions and then take note of any distracting verbal mannerisms, such as *ummm, like,* and *you know.* Practice eliminating these non-words from your responses.

Showing professionalism in an interview is all about respect for and sensitivity to others. If you cannot demonstrate that in an interview situation, why would any employer believe you would be professional, respectful, and considerate of others in any situation?

What Is Your Body Language Saying?

Job Seeker's Story

Gerard was an accomplished Finance Director who had been overlooked for promotions repeatedly over eight years. In frustration, Gerard decided he would begin to "test the waters" for a new financial management position. To help him prepare, Gerard enlisted the services of Deb, a professional career coach who advised him regarding his résumé and cover letter. Gerard was pleasantly surprised to quickly land an interview with his new résumé. Because it had been eight years since he last interviewed, Gerard immediately scheduled an appointment with Deb to do some interview coaching.

Deb suggested that they do a role-play of an interview and videotape it, so Gerard could better analyze his performance and answers. After Deb had asked two behavior-based interview questions and gotten Gerard's responses, she noticed a distracting mannerism that Gerard exhibited. After four more questions, she was perplexed to find the mannerism was constant.

Fortunately, in the videotape replay, Deb was able to point out Gerard's disconcerting mannerism. Every time Gerard was thinking about his response to a question, his eyes dropped downwards to the interviewer's (Deb's) chest. Though this might not be a problem with male interviewers, female interviewers would likely find Gerard's lengthy "chest-eying" behavior to be very offensive. Gerard had been totally oblivious to this mannerism, but concluded it might have played a role in his lack of promotions, as his two immediate supervisors (both Vice Presidents) were female.

Job Seeker's Stumble

Gerard's initial professional appearance and demeanor would seem to ensure that he lacked any distracting or off-putting nervous habits or quirks. Yet, such was not the case. Because mannerisms are unconscious, we do not see them ourselves. Studies have shown that physiology (body language, eye contact, grooming, handshake, and attire) accounts for 55 percent of any communication; actual words account for only 7 percent; and tonality (speed, temp, pitch, and tone) accounts for 38 percent. Consequently, physical mannerisms can have a powerful and decisive impact in an interview.

Job Seeker's ≥New Strategy≤

Because non-verbal behavior can greatly block or reinforce the impact of your interview communications, it is important to evaluate your non-verbal behavior for consistency with your message. When the non-verbal message is at odds with the verbal message, this is called a *mixed message.* In every instance of a mixed message, the non-verbal message is the one your interviewer will believe.

The first step in altering any physical mannerism or behavior (not based in a physical disorder) is awareness. By obtaining feedback from others, or, as Gerard did when he scrutinized a videotaped interview simulation, you can begin to grasp which nervous or repetitive habits are unproductive. Even more important, you can determine what emotions, such as anxiety, confusion, and fear, tend to bring them out. Some examples of negative mannerisms to avoid in an interview include:

> Fidgeting, twirling hair or jewelry, rocking, and leg shaking.

> Tapping or drumming fingers, wringing hands, and steepling fingers.

> Shuffling notes, and pen/pencil chewing.

> Humming, "umm-ing," and repetitive language (for example, "you know").

> Excessive use of hands while talking, rubbing hands, and jingling change.

> Finger pointing or jamming, fist pounding, and waving finger.

> Rapid blinking, staring into the distance, bored expression, and yawning.

> Wetting lips, clearing throat, biting lips, and covering mouth when speaking.

> Scratching, ear tugging, stroking nose or chin, and head tilting.

> Repeatedly cleaning eyeglasses, and looking over rim of glasses.

> Inappropriate or excessive smiling or laughing.

> Looking down or off in the distance rather than looking someone in the eyes.

> Leaning in too far (anything closer than 1.5 feet is considered "intimate").

After evaluating and isolating your negative mannerisms or quirks, the second step is cultivating replacement behaviors. For example, if you are a "hand talker," try instead to steady your hands in your lap or on your legs. If you tend to fidget with a pen or pencil, keep nothing in your hands. If you repeatedly clean your eyeglasses, consider getting contact lenses. Determine which emotions elicit your negative mannerisms and strive to eliminate or reduce the onset of those emotions in the interview.

The final step is developing powerful body language that positively reinforces your message and image. This means lots of practice in being enthusiastic, knowledgeable, and likeable. Lean in slightly to look attentive (don't slouch), smile, and look the interviewer in the eye (but not constantly). Practice relaying your answers with persuasiveness and assertiveness.

A relaxed demeanor accompanied by a firm, well-modulated voice and appropriate gestures to emphasize key points will signal your professionalism and credibility.

Plan Ahead for a Successful Interview Experience
Job Seeker's Story

Jane had seven years of experience assisting government candidates with their job searches, but was getting tired of the lengthy commute to work. She kept an eye out for positions that would be satisfying but closer to home. Eventually, she spotted an opening for a Career Counselor at a private college. Jane felt the position perfectly aligned with her skills and her interest in helping others. Apparently the Director of Career Services had the same opinion, as Jane was called in for an interview.

Jane took care to prepare for the interview. She researched the college online and prepared an attaché case with extra copies of her résumé and samples of her more outstanding work. Because she had never been to the college, she printed out directions from Mapquest and planned on leaving one hour early to ensure she arrived on time.

The day of the interview arrived, and Jane had high hopes. Her Mapquest directions indicated a route via a nearby tollway. This route was half the distance of her usual commute to her current job. As she merged onto the tollway, Jane noticed the traffic was especially heavy. Within the next 45 minutes Jane was nearly sideswiped by a taxi and almost missed her exit maneuvering through dense traffic. By the time she arrived at the college, she was shaken and disturbed. Although the route was half the mileage of her usual commute, it had taken her nearly as long with a lot more anxiety.

As Jane interviewed with the Director of Career Services, she couldn't seem to shake her negative experience on the tollway. Trying to appear enthusiastic, Jane summoned up a smile occasionally but wondered if her commute would be harrowing every day. The interviewer must have sensed Jane's hesitant mood: At one point she remarked, *"We are looking for someone who really wants to be here."* Jane assured her she did, but felt queasiness in her stomach. Could her nerves really handle the daily stressful commute? Jane really wasn't sure.

Jane did not get a job offer. Although she had said the right words, her concern and discomfort over her commute showed in the interview. Weeks later, Jane discovered there was an alternate route to the college that had much less traffic.

Job Seeker's Stumble

Overall, Jane prepared well for the interview by doing her research, getting her marketing materials ready, and obtaining directions to the interview site. But she neglected to verify those directions by doing a "test run." Instead, she had naively trusted the online directions without realizing that, though the distance was shorter, heavy commuting traffic could make the trip almost as long as her present commute at twice the distance. The additional stress-induced factors of the commuting ordeal shook Jane's composure and distracted her throughout the interview. How different her outcome might have been had she sought alternate routes to the college!

Job Seeker's ≥New Strategy≤

Getting to an interview safely and with the least amount of anxiety possible is the ideal for anyone who interviews. You cannot afford to have stressful events crowding out your thoughtful preparation for the interview or wreaking havoc with your composure, attention, and body-language signals that should be reinforcing your message, rather than at odds with it.

Preparing for an interview involves more than simply practicing your interview responses. By attending to a few practical considerations in advance, you can optimize your entire interview experience. These interview-preparation elements include:

▷ **Transportation:** Always arrange a backup plan regarding your mode of transportation. Check out your vehicle ahead of time to ensure it is in proper working order. Research bus schedules and look into taxi services to determine alternate transportation. If you are flying or taking a train to an interview, plan enough time in the schedule as a cushion should the flight or train be delayed. Wherever possible, do a test run of the route during the same hours that you would be using to get to the interview to assess how early you need to leave.

▷ **Directions and Parking:** Obtain alternate directions and do a test run to determine the optimum route. Ask the person who scheduled your interview for parking directions and any special instructions, including reimbursement arrangements (if any) for travel and parking. You do not want to end up parking illegally and have your car towed away while you are in the interview!

▷ **Weather:** Look into the weather forecasts as the interview date approaches so you can make needed adjustments in travel time to the interview. Weather will also affect your choice of clothing and what you choose to bring with you, such as an umbrella or snow boots.

▷ **Interview Outfit:** Select and ready your interview outfit at least one day before the interview. This includes all your clothing and outerwear, shoes, jewelry (keep to a minimum), and portfolio/attaché case that will hold your job search marketing materials (extra résumés, reference lists, and examples of your work). Be mindful of the professional attire customary for the interview situation. If you are not sure, check it out ahead of time by visiting the workplace prior to your interview. Do not make the mistake of appraising normal work attire on "casual Friday."

▷ **Interviewers:** At the time you schedule the interview, ask for the names of all the interviewers who will be seeing you and their positions with the company. Try to determine if it will be one large group interview or individual serial interviews throughout the day. If you are expected to stay the whole day to be interviewed you certainly need to know that.

▷ **Organizational Chart, Job Description, and Media Folder:** From the interview scheduler, request a copy of the organizational chart, job description for the position, and media folder or press kit, and do that as politely as possible. You could ask to have them mailed to you, or use this as an opportunity to do a test run by offering to pick up the materials. Realize that you are making "extra work" for the scheduler, so do whatever is necessary to make it easy to comply with your request. The organizational chart will help you to better understand the layers within the company and your potential department/division. It may even include the names of some of your interviewers! The full job description is essential in planning interview responses that highlight the skills actually needed in the job. Finally, the media folder typically contains press releases and other PR materials that serve as background information for media who want to run a news story on the company. You may not obtain all of these elements, but asking for them will indicate your thoroughness and professionalism. It will undoubtedly impress the interview scheduler, who may in turn relay that information to the interviewers.

▷ **Research:** Do some digging online, at the library, and through your social network into the company and industry so you can appear knowledgeable and interested in this particular position with this company. Also, find out information about the interviewer(s); you may discover points of similarity in their backgrounds that align with yours. Perhaps you belonged to the same fraternity, attended the same college, or volunteered for the same community causes. You will surely want to mention that in the interview.

One final note: Even if you are fully prepared you can still undermine your interview prospects by arriving too early. If you get to an interview more than 10 minutes early, and you know where you are going in the building, then bide your time. Sit in your car or drive around the block. Review your research and recall the primary interview points you want to make. Do whatever it takes to use up the extra time. Do not impose on your potential employer by arriving far too early. You have an appointment time for a reason; heed it.

Weaknesses: The $64,000 (or More) Question

Job Seeker's Story

Randy, an Engineering Technician, had been unemployed for more than a year. Although he had gotten several interviews over that period of time, none of them transitioned into second interviews or job offers. Randy was perplexed, but attributed his job search track record to strong competition and a struggling economy.

When Randy was contacted about an interview with a mid-sized company his hopes were renewed. The interview was scheduled for the next day with the Human Resources (HR) Manager, so Randy spent his time researching the company, its background, and its products. He took copious notes and reviewed them the morning of his interview. As Randy got ready to go, he felt sure he would make a great impression with his knowledge about the company.

The HR Manager was indeed duly impressed. He even commented about the thoroughness of Randy's information, including a recent press release that the interviewer had not yet seen. The interview seemed to be going well. Then the HR Manager asked, *"What would your boss say are your weaknesses?"*

Randy immediately responded, *"My boss would tell you I have no weaknesses. I am the best of the best, the cream of the crop."*

With that response Randy settled back, quite pleased because there would be nothing to blemish his candidacy. The interviewer jotted down a note, without replying. Then the HR Manager asked another question: *"What do you think your weaknesses are?"*

Randy was getting irritated by this line of questioning. Why would he want to admit to any weaknesses? That seemed counter-productive. It did seem strange, he thought, that on almost every interview he got asked this question. Interviewers were surely not choosing candidates based on their weaknesses, were they? With these thoughts running through his mind, Randy answered, *"I would agree with my boss. I am the best of the best. In fact, engineers at different levels have come to me for advice and guidance."*

As the HR Manager made note of Randy's comment, he responded, *"If you are that good, how is it that you have been out of work for over a year?"*

Randy shook his head and mumbled, *"I don't know."*

The interview ended abruptly after this exchange, and Randy did not hear from this interviewer or the company again.

Job Seeker's Stumble

Randy's assertion that he had no weaknesses, either perceived by himself or his former boss, strained believability. Every job seeker has weaknesses, and to claim "perfection" raises red flags about an inflated ego or, at the very least, lack of self-awareness. Compounding the claim of no weaknesses, Randy appeared to be irritated and defiant when answering these two questions. Apparently, Randy had not done his research well enough. If he had, he would have discovered the "weakness" question is very typically asked by interviewers, and perhaps he would have prepared far better answers.

Job Seeker's ≥New Strategy≤

Knowing that possible questioning about weaknesses could happen in the interview, strive to appear appropriately human and humble by admitting a weakness in such a way as to lessen the negative impact on your candidacy. In any case, you and your former supervisor should agree on one weakness you will discuss with interviewers. Here are some alternative categories of weaknesses Randy could have used, as well as strategies for handling the "weakness" interview question:

▷ **Not Relevant:** Select a weakness that has no bearing on the job. Carefully review the job description to become familiar with needed skills and strengths for the position. Then pick a weakness that has no involvement with the job. For example, Randy might have said, "*I am not as strong as I might be in dealing with international customers, since all of my past experience has been with local and regional customers. That's an area I would be eager to learn.*" In his research Randy had ascertained that this company was regional in scope, with no immediate plans for international growth.

▷ **Needs Improvement:** Choose a skill or knowledge area that you feel needs improvement, but be sure it is not a critical one for the job. Then talk about what you are doing to get better. Thus, Randy's response could have been, "*My computer skills involving Microsoft Excel were a bit out-of-date, so I took two courses at the local community college in the latest version of Excel, as well as the Advanced Excel class.*"

▷ **Already Apparent:** If you are lacking one of the requirements or a preferred/optional requirement for the position and this is already apparent to the interviewer via your résumé and your interview responses, do what you can to lessen the impact of this "missing" requirement. For example, Randy could have used this diversion statement: "*I feel my weakness at this point is that I have a bachelor's degree and you prefer a master's degree. However, if I may review some of my accomplishments with you, I believe you will see that I have the real-world experience equivalent of master's-level knowledge.*"

> ▷ **Strength as a Weakness:** Disguising a strength as a weakness is probably the least effective strategy, as it has been overused by so many applicants. But, if this is a true weakness that you and your supervisor have agreed on, you can authentically claim it. Randy's thoroughness was an actual weakness, but he could have talked about this weakness this way: *"I tend to be very thorough with the projects I am leading or participating in, and sometimes that means it takes longer than anticipated. However, I have always been complimented by customers for my attention to detail and quality. I have even won quality awards in the past."*

Any one of these types of responses to the "weakness" question should put you in better standing than Randy's answers did. Avoid mentioning skills and knowledge that are essential in the performance of the job for which you are applying—at all costs. You do not need to supply the interviewer with reasons for appropriately screening you out!

Interview Responses Need to Hit the Employer's Target

Job Seeker's Story

Tina, a high school graduate, had worked in retail sales for two years and decided to transition into a clerical job so she could have regular work hours similar to her friends. Her ultimate goal was to be a Clerk Typist in a public-sector job. She was experienced with business word-processing and spreadsheet software, but Tina's typing speed was well under the 45 words-per-minute (wpm) requirement in order to apply for such a position. Consequently, out of desperation, she decided to apply for anything she could find in the want ads until she could land a clerical job and build her typing skills.

Tina's strategy paid off immediately. She located a want-ad announcement for a grocery store Cashier Clerk position at a large food chain in a nearby town. When she saw the high union wages mentioned in the ad, she went to the store and applied on the spot. Within one hour she had an interview with Jessica, the Human Resources Manager.

As Tina responded to Jessica's questions about her past retail job, she was beginning to imagine what she would do with her wages and how she would still have time to conduct a continued job search for a clerical job. Tina felt the interview was proceeding nicely when Jessica asked, *"Where do you see yourself in five years?"*

Tina immediately and proudly answered, *"I plan on being a Clerk Typist with the City of Oakland."*

To Tina's utter bewilderment, the interviewer suddenly lost interest in her and ended the interview. Tina did not get a job offer. She had no idea why she had not been offered the job.

Job Seeker's Stumble

No matter the level of position, employers seek to hire applicants who will stay with the company as long as possible. Talent retention and talent development are very real issues for companies. In fact, according to the 2007 CareerXRoads Annual Sources of Hire Survey, a survey of a representative cross-section of companies and recruiters, internal transfers and promotions accounted for 33.9 percent of open positions filled. This source of hire (internal employees) was the top-ranked method for filling companies' open positions. Consequently, indicating in an interview BEFORE you are even hired that you have no intention of staying with the company does not make you a viable candidate in the employment reviewer's eyes.

Job Seeker's ⋚New Strategy⋚

The employer's target—his or her needs and concerns—need to be uppermost in your thoughts as you respond to interview questions. Not only the content of your message, but also the manner of delivery, has to "connect" with the interviewer both rationally and emotionally. A rational connection is one that reassures the employer concerning his or her needs (such as your ability to do the job well and produce results), as well as his or her concerns (such as your willingness to commit to the company and be loyal if given the opportunity for training and promotion). An emotional connection with the interviewer elicits rapport, confidence, and believability—all necessary factors in the final job-offer decision.

Using the *"Where do you want to be in five years?"* question, here is a three-step approach Tina could have used to respond that would have bolstered her candidacy:

1. **Inform:** Providing information (details) is rational. It allows the employment reviewer to "know" the facts. You provide the logical facts in the interview. Some are short answers to questions such as *"What was your GPA?"* or more detail-backed C-C-A-R stories to validate your skills and accomplishments. Most interviewees do not move beyond this step in their interview answers. For this step Tina could have said, *"My plan is to stay with a company, such as yours, where I can develop my professional skills and grow as the company grows."*

2. **Persuade:** This is a rational and emotional step. Using quantifiers, for example, strengthens the factual (rational) content of your message and makes it more convincing (emotional). You are, in essence, bolstering your "story" to persuade the listener that you are to be believed—that you do possess the needed skills, strengths, attributes, and experiences to be the best hire possible. Weave in numbers, dollar amounts, and percentages to characterize your factual information, which in turn will boost your credibility. For example, Tina could have continued her response by saying, *"Over the course of five years I would hope to improve my skill sets and take on more responsibility. Since I have led retail-sales teams of up to five employees to achieve record-breaking sales, I would like the opportunity to move into a team leadership role."*

The delivery of your message can also serve to persuade the employment reviewer to "like" you as a candidate. If Tina had mirrored some of the interviewer's behavior, such as energy level, rate of speech, body posture, and eye contact, she would have "connected" with Jessica and made a more favorable impression. The likability factor plays a big role in the final decision. If two candidates possess equal qualifications and accomplishments, it is the more likable candidate (perhaps seen as fitting better into the team and company culture) who will be viewed as the superior candidate.

3. **Motivate:** This final step is totally emotional. In it you are attempting to get the employment reviewer (interviewer) to take action and make a decision that you desire—inclusion in the next round of interviewing or even extending a generous offer, for example. To round out her answer, Tina might have commented, *"Since I have up-to-date computer skills along with two years of customer-service experience, I believe I could start immediately with very little training needed. How soon would you like to see this position filled?"* Tina is clearly supplying the interviewer with the bottom-line logical reasons (saving time and money) for curtailing the rest of the interview schedule with other applicants and hiring her as soon as possible.

This three-step strategy incorporates both the rational and emotional components that are a part of the interviewer's decision-making process, whether conscious or not. By addressing both components successfully you will reinforce what is ultimately an emotional decision—based on likability, culture fit, and personal branding—with rational, logical reasons to hire you instead of other candidates. The key concept to remember is that people "buy" because of emotion and justify their decision based on logic. This holds true for interviewers as well; after all, they are human too!

Don't Ever Let Them See You Sweat

Job Seeker's Story

Jennifer found herself in an interview with two people, Margaret and Pierce, for the Contract Negotiator position with Pac-Lat. Pierce took the lead in the interview, rapidly firing questions at her, grunting at her answers, interrupting her, and rolling his eyes. He seemed doubtful and unimpressed with her as a candidate. At the same time, Margaret was warm, shaking her head at Pierce, and telling Jennifer not to worry about it.

Jennifer found herself directing her answers more and more toward Margaret and all but ignoring Pierce's questions. Her irritation with Pierce was quite evident and eventually he sat back to watch as Jennifer opened up to Margaret as if they were old friends, answering each of her questions.

After the interview, Margaret and Pierce discussed Jennifer and decided she was not going to be very successful at handling the stress and pressure of the position because she had done such a poor job in handling the stress brought on by one arrogant and rude interviewer. If she could not handle that, how would she ever handle the critical multi-million-dollar contract negotiations? Because of this, she was not offered the job.

Job Seeker's Stumble

Jennifer was lured into what is referred to as "good cop, bad cop" in the interviewing (and law enforcement) world. This same scenario can be played in a panel interview or with just one rude or harsh interviewer; the idea is that a job seeker should never let the interviewer see him or her sweat or realize that he or she (the interviewer) is getting to him or her. If Jennifer cracks under the pressure of the interview, she certainly demonstrates that it will not take much to upset her in the workplace.

Job Seeker's ≷New Strategy≷

First, don't be fooled: The nice interviewer is no more your friend then the not-so-nice one. This is a ploy! Do not be tricked into becoming conspiratorial toward the nice one and irritable toward the mean one. Keep your cool, be professional, and answer each one with the same level of professionalism, regardless of how they treat you. Do not let yourself become heated or argumentative with the bad cop, but also do not feel safe in telling the good cop anything he or she asks. Again, the interviewer is not your "friend," but rather someone evaluating you for the job.

If you feel overwhelmed, take a deep breath, and avoid becoming flustered. If questions are being launched at you too quickly, say something along the lines of, *"Let's see, I believe you asked me.... I'll address that question before I get to the next."* or *"Just a moment. Let me answer his question first."*

As with all interviews with more than one person, before leaving the interview, make sure you learn each person's title and name because you will want to write each of them thank-you letters, no matter how any one of them made you feel.

Now that you have survived the interview you can decide whether a company that would allow this kind of interviewing is a place where you would want to work or not. The individuals involved in the game might be people you would have no interaction with in the future, or they could be representative of the type of organization in which you would work. If you have not done your homework on the company yet, now would be a good time to learn more about it. If the opportunity leads to a second interview, be sure to ask to meet the team with whom you would work and to inquire about what happened to the last person in the role. (Was he or she promoted? Terminated? Relocated?)

Remember: It is an interview, and that is a test in which to prove you can handle stress and challenges.

Dress to Fit the Industry, Organization, and Culture

Job Seeker's Story

Sanelle had the opportunity to interview for the position of Manager for the Kidz Play Hut. She had visited The Hut and knew that all the staff wore running shorts and had to constantly be in the play area, but she reasoned that, for a Manager's position, she should still wear a nice suit to make a positive impression.

When Sanelle arrived, she had dressed with extreme professionalism, wearing a navy blue suit, designer scarf, and navy pumps. She was interviewed by a young woman of similar age who was wearing running shorts. The interview had hardly progressed when the interviewer said, *"You know, if you are looking for a 9–5 office job where you can wear your fancy suits, then this is not the place for you."*

Sanelle tried to convince the interviewer that her record spoke for itself. She had worked in similar game rooms, movie theaters, and other kids play places where shorts were a must. She explained she was unafraid of getting dirty and being hands-on. However, the interviewer maintained a skeptical impression and did not warm to Sanelle throughout the rest of the interview.

At the end of the interview, the employer was not convinced that Sanelle would fit in. She could not get past the suit or how out of place it was in the Kidz Play Hut. She believed that Sanelle would not have dressed that way if it was not how she wanted to dress on the job. As a result, she did not offer Sanelle the job.

Job Seeker's Stumble

In Sanelle's effort to make a good impression, she positioned herself right out of a job opportunity. Although it seems that it would make sense to always dress professionally, her experience is just one example of the job seeker just not fitting into the company or the culture based on her choice of attire.

Job Seeker's ⋛New Strategy⋚

To make a positive impression, you should dress to fit in to the organization and its culture. In order to do this, you need to learn how they dress. If you do not have contacts at the organization, you might talk to your network, or you might perform a little reconnaissance work by parking across the street from the company to see how the personnel are dressed as they arrive in the morning. However, be careful with "casual Fridays," when staff may be dressed down compared to the rest of the week.

Another way to possibly gain insight on how to dress is to ask the person who is scheduling your interview: *"Is there anything special I should be prepared for during this interview?"* When asked for clarification, you might state that you just wanted to be prepared if you needed several hours for a series of interviews or if you might be expecting a tour of the plant where you should adjust what you are wearing for safety. This information could provide subtle clues about how to dress.

Consider the following professional attire do's and don'ts:

For Professional Organizations or Job Fairs

▷ Keep it simple. The best colors for men's suits are charcoal gray, dark blue, and black. In today's business world, three-piece suits are overkill and should be avoided. Women have many more choices in acceptable colors, but should aim for a knee-length skirt and not a miniskirt. Red or other fiery, aggressive colors should be avoided by both men and women.

▷ Pay attention to your shoes and polish them.

▷ Select a muted tie (men) or simple jewelry and minimal accessories (women), because you want the attention to be on you and what you say, and not your great accessories.

For Semi-Professional Organizations

▷ In most cases the suit is still your best bet. For men, if it looks as if you are overdressed, you can remove your jacket and even your tie. Women might opt for a more casual suit, or a jacket and trousers.

For Casual Organizations

▷ Avoid wearing jeans, even if that is how the staff at the company is dressed. Instead, strive to dress professionally without overdressing; a nice pair of dark or casual slacks and a sports shirt will allow men to make a nice presentation. Women could wear a nice dress, blouse and skirt, or blouse and trousers.

▷ Shoes are still important, and a nice loafer-style dress shoe for men or a simple closed-toe flat or pump for women would be appropriate.

Additional Tips

▷ Remove all facial jewelry (unless they are industry/job appropriate).

▷ Get a haircut.

▷ Keep hair simple, clean, and professional.

▷ Trim or shave facial hair.

▷ Remove pinky rings, and keep jewelry simple with one or two rings per hand. For women, stick with one pair of earrings (none for men).

▷ Place gold chains inside of your shirt and wear only one.

▷ Clean and trim nails.

▷ Wear dark socks with dark trousers.

▷ Avoid shimmery or sheer fabrics.

▷ Wear simple and minimal accessories.

▷ Conceal tattoos (unless they are industry/job appropriate).

Dress for the company to show you fit in with the organization, its people, and culture, and they will see you as one of their own.

CHAPTER 9

Slippery Salary Slopes

∧

Keep Your Salary Expectations Current

Job Seeker's Story

After 10 years as a stay-at-home mom, Alice decided to return to work full-time. She was a Registered Nurse and had been working part-time as a volunteer Emergency Medical Technician for a small, local fire district. Concerned about the length of time that had elapsed since she worked as an RN, Alice wondered whether she would even be considered a viable candidate.

Due to her concerns, Alice decided to hire a career coach to help her in preparing for interviews. In a role-playing session with the coach, Mina, she was asked what she expected in pay. Not anticipating this question, Alice blurted out, *"I was thinking maybe $12–13 per hour. It's been so long since I worked that I would need to catch up on the new technology."*

In response, Mina asked, *"Alice, do you have any idea what the going rate is for a nurse these days?"*

She said, *"Apparently not; what is it?"*

The coach replied, *"At least $19–30 per hour in this geographic area."*

Alice's immediate retort was, *"Oh, I don't think they would ever pay me that."*

The coach advised Alice not to bring up salary at the interview, but wait until the interviewer did. Knowing what the possible going rate could be, Alice was to ask the interviewer what range they were offering and where the interviewer saw her in that range.

At the interview, Alice followed the coach's advice and nearly fell out of her chair when she heard the interviewer ask, "*Alice, we'd like to get you on board quickly. Do you think you could start next week at $30 per hour?*" Alice realized she had more than doubled her salary before even starting the job by following the coach's skillful negotiating advice.

Job Seeker's Stumble

Alice did not realize the current demand for nursing services in her area or know the going rate of pay for RNs at the local hospital where she had her interview. Because of this lack of information, she very nearly under-priced herself by a substantial amount in the salary negotiations phase of the interview.

Job Seeker's ⋝New Strategy⋜

Before going on any interview, do your research on the going rate of pay for the type of position, the years of experience, the industry, and the geographic location. These are all variables that affect the rate of pay to a significant degree.

Start by investigating salary comparison sites online (such as Salary.com and Payscale.com). These will yield figures to help you determine a ballpark range. Then, informational interview with others in the field to find out not only the going rate, but also the benefits typically included in a total compensation package. Do not assume it is the same with all organizations in the industry. As Alice discovered, do not assume it has stayed the same as it was 10 years ago!

Making Demands Can Leave You Without an Offer

Job Seeker's Story

Yvonne, a Retail Sales Professional, had the chance to go to the next level in her career by interviewing with a very upscale retailer. She breezed through two interviews and received an offer. The interviewer proudly offered Yvonne $10 an hour. Shocked at what she felt was a low offer, Yvonne did not ask any questions, but asked for time to consider the offer.

She went home to discuss it with her husband, who told her to tell the employer that she could not accept the job for less than $15 an hour. Yvonne called the employer and smartly asked for a time to meet to discuss the offer.

In the meeting, Yvonne confidently expressed her requirement for $15 an hour. In response, the interviewer did not hesitate to thank her for her time and to tell her that he was rescinding the offer. Surprised, Yvonne said, *"You're rescinding the offer? Aren't we supposed to negotiate or at least talk about other compensation options?"*

In response he said, *"While we might have found some common ground, we are not looking for someone who makes demands or is unrealistic about wages for the retail market. Since I know your demands, I realize we cannot meet them and even if you were to agree to a lower number, I have to expect you would not be happy and you would not stay with the company long."*

Yvonne took her bruised ego home with the realization that she needed to learn more about negotiation.

Job Seeker's Stumble

Instead of negotiating the offer to achieve a possible win-win, Yvonne lost the opportunity by giving an ultimatum that was unrealistic in terms of the employer's budget. Her requirement left no room for negotiation, so the employer rescinded the offer in favor of another candidate who would fit in its range and therefore be more likely to stay longer with the company.

Job Seeker's ≷New Strategy≷

You should never give an employer an ultimatum or absolute regarding salary! They call the process salary *negotiation* for a reason. If you find yourself being offered less than you were expecting, attempt to explore options with the employer. When negotiating, it is important to be face-to-face.

First, thank the interviewer for the offer, state that you are very interested in working for the company, and ask if the base is at all negotiable. If it is, do not say what you are looking for, but instead ask what more they would be willing to do for you, based on the track record of performance you bring to the company.

If you are told that the base is not negotiable, do not quit yet! Now is the time to investigate others options that might better fit the employer's budget. Ask if the company would consider quarterly reviews with performance bonuses or another form of performance-based compensation.

Always remember that almost everything is negotiable, so avoid making demands and instead make inquiries. Sometimes it can take hearing "no" to the first several options before you hear "yes," but you will never know until you pose the question.

Ask and You Shall Receive More Salary

Job Seeker's Story

After graduating with her master's degree, Carolyn interviewed with a large telecommunications company and accepted the position at the time of the offer. During her first year she worked extremely hard and made numerous outstanding contributions to the company, some of which even resulted in awards and accolades. In fact, not a day went by that her boss was not praising her and her customers were not thanking her.

When she came up for her one-year review, her boss proudly told her she received the company's largest increase that year (67 cents an hour). Carolyn was very disappointed, but this was only the beginning. Later, during a coffee break, when she discussed the matter of raises with a co-worker, she learned that the last person in her role had started at $15,000 more annually than she had. She calculated that at an average raise of 67 cents per year it would take her more than 10 years just to get to where her predecessor started, and that she would lose more than $150,000 in salary she could have earned over those years.

Not one to give up, Carolyn approached her boss to learn about opportunities to move up with the company, assuming she could increase her salary in that manner. She left the meeting deflated after learning that it was company policy to never exceed a 3-percent salary increase for any internal company promotion. She now realized that, even if she got promoted out of the job she loved, she would always be behind the curve on company salaries.

Job Seeker's Stumble

Carolyn thought that if she worked hard she would be rewarded. However, because she did not negotiate up front, she would either have to seek promotions or leave the company to increase her salary significantly. In fact, she would have more of a chance of increasing her salary with this firm by leaving and later reapplying and negotiating the second time around.

Job Seeker's ≥New Strategy≥

Never make the mistake of accepting the first salary offer that you receive. In fact, it has been said that, if the job seeker says the dollar amount first, it is the ceiling (or the highest offer you will receive), and, if the employer says the dollar amount first, it is the floor (or the lowest offer you will receive).

When you receive an offer, thank the employer, ask if there are other elements to consider (perks, benefits, and/or bonuses), and then ask for time to consider the offer. It is not unreasonable to ask for up to a week.

When you again meet with the employer, tell him that you have thought it over, that you greatly appreciate the offer, and would like to know if the base salary is negotiable. *Always* start with the base. Don't expend the initial, valuable energy on negotiating benefits yet. Consider these two outcomes of asking if the position is negotiable:

Example A

Employer: *"I'm sorry, but $33,000 is the highest we have allotted for that position."*

Job Seeker: *"I can understand that, but what if you were to put me under another title in a position, where I could serve these needs as well as some of the additional areas I am skilled in?"*

Be specific or talk about a project/goal. Focus on redirecting the job description to put it in a higher salary bracket.

Example B

Job Seeker: *"I truly appreciate the offer, but was wondering if it is negotiable."*

Employer: *"What did you have in mind?"*

Job Seeker: *"Well, I'm still flexible, but I was hoping that you might make a higher offer based on the value (skills, etc.) that I am offering you. Is that possible?"*

Employer: *"That's usually our standing offer for this position."* or *"The most I can offer you is $38,000."*

Obviously, with the first answer, you will have to sell yourself into another bracket. In Example B, you have to tread lightly. Is this a situation where you have to jump to Example A, or are you happy with $38,000? If you are okay with $38,000 but would like a little more, perhaps you should now talk about other options, such as mileage reimbursement or increased vacation time.

Sometimes you just have to walk away; don't beat yourself up if you can't get a reasonable offer. It happens. Conversely, more often than not you can increase your salary by $15,000 or more just by asking if the offer is negotiable.

Avoid Locking Yourself Into a Low Salary

Job Seeker's Story

Beth had recently graduated from a prestigious MBA program with top grades and was thrilled to have the opportunity to interview with her number-one choice of firms, The Alcor Company. The interview with Ms. Salsbury, VP of Marketing, was going well until she asked Beth about what kind of salary she was seeking.

Beth rapidly recalled that her classmates were receiving offers from the low 50s to the high 80s, and without hesitation decided it was smart and safe to put herself in the middle of the range. So, she told the employer, *"I am looking for around $65,000 to start."* The interviewer thanked Beth and told her that she would get back to her shortly.

A few days later Beth was invited back in and offered $63,000 to join the company. She was surprised they had offered her the low end of the going range with all that she had to offer. It was even less than what she asked for! But Beth felt that she was in no position to negotiate because she had thrown out the first offer.

Disappointed, Beth accepted the offer, which she would regret during the next year as her colleagues told her about the offers they had negotiated for themselves.

Job Seeker's Stumble

Beth's error is that she limited her options by naming a dollar figure. Even if the employer might have considered offering her $80,000, he would not consider offering more than $65,000 now.

Job Seeker's ≳New Strategy≲

You can easily avoid pigeon-holing yourself to a specific dollar amount by answering the question of salary with a more open-ended answer such as one of the following:

"I am negotiable; what do you have allotted for the position?"

or

"I am confident that if we agree I am the right choice for the position, we will be able to come to an equitable arrangement for salary, wouldn't you agree?"

Each of these responses deflects the question and allows you to lob the offer back over into the interviewer's court.

Sometimes, however, the interviewer will push you to commit to a specific dollar figure. If that is the case, you might try:

"As I explained before, at this point I really don't feel I have enough information to commit to a dollar amount. However, based on my knowledge of salary ranges for this position and my personal salary requirements, I am expecting the position pays between $50 and 85K."

or

"I'd prefer to leave this topic until we're more certain about my appropriateness for this position. However, I am expecting that the position will be somewhere in the $50–80K range."

Should the interviewer ultimately offer you the low end of your range, you should be prepared to negotiate and prove your worth by demonstrating the value you can bring to the company. By knowing the salary ranges for the position and answering in a way that allows you to keep your options open, you will have a stronger position from which to get the salary offer you desire.

Salary Research Pays Off

Job Seeker's Story

Victoria had decided to move from the Midwest to Maryland to be geographically closer to her mother and sisters. She anticipated her job search would go well as there seemed to be lots of demand for Customer Service Representatives in the tech support industry. Victoria had moved up the career ladder in her previous job; she was getting lots of overtime pay, and had a very competitive health benefits package worth 30 percent of her base salary.

At her first interview in Maryland, Victoria was asked early on about how much per hour she had made at her last job. Without blinking an eye, she told the interviewer her hourly base salary and asked to be considered for a similar salary. The interviewer seemed pleased and, within 40 minutes, made a job offer that matched Victoria's previous salary, which she accepted.

Unfortunately, Victoria quickly learned when her first paycheck arrived that she would have to make severe adjustments in her lifestyle to accommodate her now-reduced income level. Though she was happy to have made her job change, she wondered what she could have done to improve her financial compensation with her new employer.

Job Seeker's Stumble

Victoria did not factor a couple of critical items into her salary expectations: Her new position did not allow for overtime opportunities (which had accounted for 25 percent over her base pay in her previous job) and the health-benefits package was not as robust (higher deductibles and limited coverage). In addition, Victoria had moved to a geographic region with significant cost-of-living differences from the Midwest.

Job Seeker's ≷New Strategy≶

If Victoria had considered the value of the total compensation package she was leaving behind, and had done some research about salary and compensation levels for her profession in Maryland, she might have fared far better. Here are some steps Victoria could have taken:

▹ Establish a current total compensation benchmark, including base salary, overtime pay, and benefits package value.

ow with a cost-of-living and salary comparison for the two geographic regions you are comparing, such as the Midwest and East Coast. Some general online salary comparison and industry salary sites include Salary.com, Payscale.com, and Salaryexpert.com. For profession-specific salary survey guides you can access the Jobstar Salary Guide or the Vault Salary and Compensation Survey. For customized salary notifications (via RSS feeds) based on specific search parameters, go to Salaryscout. In addition, the Bureau of Labor Statistics (*www.bls.gov*) keeps employment information by industry, occupation, and region.

▹ Conduct a Google search based on a search string containing the name of your profession or job title and the search term *salaries.* (For example, Victoria could have used the search string "customer service" + "salaries.")

▹ Network with others in your field to research and verify more local salary and benefits information. For example, you can ask discreetely at chapter and annual meetings of professional associations, professional-development seminars, and social groups, and online at professional business networking sites such as LinkedIn.com. Bear in mind that most people do not want to divulge what they personally make, but would be willing to discuss a "typical salary range and benefits" for the position and industry.

▹ Keep track of this researched information, noting the sources. The more closely the sourced information matches your own position, industry, years of experience, and geographic locale, the more likely it can be considered comparable. This will arm you with verifiable and documented research on which to estimate the market-based range that you can use in effective salary negotiations.

▹ Remember that benefits are typically more negotiable than salary. Once you've done what you can to improve the salary offered, you have the option of increasing the total compensation package through additional benefits negotiations.

CHAPTER 10

Job Reference Rejects

∧

References Need to Know What You're Doing

Job Seeker's Story

Emma had three terrific professional references. She contacted them in May to discuss the medical office positions for which she was applying and to provide an updated copy of her résumé. Her references were happy to speak with her, and updated their contact information for her references page.

However, several months later Emma got involved in volunteering in daycare at her church and decided to pursue a similar position. In her excitement and haste, she neglected to contact her references and let them know what she was doing. As a result, when they were contacted by employers seeking references, they could not effectively talk about Emma in the context of daycare professional. They shared positive information about her, but it was clear they were in the dark, and the employer sensed a strong disconnect that caused her concern about Emma as a professional candidate for the job. Ultimately, although she liked Emma very much, she chose another candidate who had stronger references.

Additionally, the references were left in an uncomfortable position. They were not looking forward to future reference checks for Emma, because she was not demonstrating the follow-through they were asked to verify by potential employers.

Job Seeker's Stumble

Emma's mistake was in not keeping her references informed of her change in job targets (and, worse, how she would be an asset for those roles). If the references had been coached, or at least been given an update on her qualifications, they would have been able to promote her for her new job target. Instead, they were left in an awkward position that ultimately lost Emma the job. Unfortunately, Emma could lose her references in the future as well.

Job Seeker's ≷New Strategy≷

When it comes to references, it is not enough to ask someone to serve as your reference and then assume that you can use that person's name for all time. Instead, you need to nurture your references by contacting them regularly to keep them abreast of changes in your job targets, education, and work history. You can do this through regular follow-up phone calls and e-mails, as well as by forwarding an updated copy of your résumé as your experience changes.

In fact, if your job targets change considerably, it might even be time to rethink your references. You should ask yourself if these are the best professionals you know for your current job target or if you should look in new areas for better references who know about the new target area of your life.

Make it easy to let your references give you a boost up in your job search by empowering them with the knowledge about your career, life, and job targets to do so.

Keep Your References Up-to-Date

Job Seeker's Story

While employed as an Accountant for 14 years, Betty had never needed to contact her references regarding a job search. That changed when Betty's employer announced a large-scale lay-off. Betty's job search skills were rusty, but she persevered, learned from her mistakes, and began getting interviews.

The first time an interviewer asked for references, Betty was actually startled and remembered that all she had was her typed list of references from 14 years ago. Rather than looking unprepared, Betty handed over the list to the interviewer and asked that he make a copy, as it was her original. Betty told herself that references weren't really all that important anyway; in fact, they were just a "formality." When she got home, Betty turned her attention to more pressing activities, such as job postings to respond to and networking meetings. Betty used the same references list for the next three interviews.

After two months went by with a total of four interviews and absolutely no response—negative or positive—from any interviewer, Betty mentioned her plight to her former supervisor, James. James wondered why she had not asked him to be a reference. Her reply was, "*I already have references. I really do not need any more.*" When James asked who these references were and Betty revealed they were all from her job of 14 years ago, James tactfully suggested she might want to reconsider her list and add more recent references. At the very least, she should contact her references to let them know she was in the job market again.

Betty took James's suggestions to heart and tried to call her three references. Unfortunately, two of them were unreachable because their phone numbers had been disconnected and they had moved. When she called her third reference's phone number, she discovered to her dismay (from her reference's son) that her "key" reference had died three years ago and the son did not appreciate being "bothered" by reference-checking employers who had called in the last two months.

Job Seeker's Stumble
Betty made two crucial mistakes regarding her references: (1) assuming that reference checking was not an important part of the hiring process, and (2) assuming that her references could be reached and would be ready and willing to comment on her qualifications.

Job Seeker's ⋛New Strategy⋚

Because the SHRM 2006 Access to Human Capital and Employment Verification Survey Report revealed that a large percentage (53 percent) of job seekers lie on their résumés, employers and recruiters are justifiably concerned about the veracity of those documents. This means reference checking has become even more critical than ever before. Without corroboration from outside sources, how is an employer to believe you really do possess the skills you claim and are a viable candidate? Reference-checking companies have proliferated in response to this hiring need; in fact, job seekers themselves can verify what their references are actually saying via services such as MyReferences.com and others.

As Betty learned, keeping in touch with your references to continually update their contact information ensures their availability to move you along in the hiring process. Without references, your chances of being advanced to a second-interview stage or landing a job offer are remote. Choose up-to-date references who can comment on your recent accomplishments and endeavors, and keep their contact information current. E-mail your résumé to them and coach them on your job target, your related skills and qualifications, and your significant points of differentiation from other candidates. Your references represent the essential corroborating evidence that the employment reviewer needs to keep you in the pool of candidates for further consideration.

Unprepared Could Mean Unemployed

Job Seeker's Story

Margaret had only worked for one employer in 13 years when she started looking for a new position at a company where she believed she would find promotional opportunities. Because she did not want her employer to know she was looking for a new job, she assumed she could not get references and just crossed her fingers that an interviewer would not ask for any.

Of course, as would be expected, the company she was most interested in asked for her references during the interview. To this request she replied, "I have only worked for one employer so I cannot provide any, since I still work there and do not want them to know I am looking." Unfortunately, this opened up the opportunity for the employer to ask more questions that Margaret was not prepared for, such as why she was looking and if she had current conflicts with her employer.

Margaret responded positively and proactively, and talked at length about the good job she had done for her employer. However, she could give no references who could support her character, experience, or accomplishments.

Margaret left the interview crestfallen and wondered how people ever got new jobs when they had only had one employer.

Job Seeker's Stumble

Poor Margaret just did not know that you must always have references, even if they do not come from an employer. She did not realize that a professional reference can represent a wide array of individuals in her professional and personal circle, or that there are creative ways to get references without hurting your current position. Without any references, it will appear to the interviewer that you must have something to hide.

Job Seeker's ≥New Strategy≤

If you have only had one employer during your career, or you are a new graduate with no work history, you can still have references. Although employers prefer employer references, they will understand if you have alternative references and an explanation.

Before discounting your current employer, take a moment to see if there are safe options you might consider. Is there another manager or supervisor other than your own with whom you have built a positive relationship? Has a manager who knows you well retired, moved to another company, or been laid off?

After considering actual company managers, explore other employer-related options such as: vendors, educators/trainers, and major customers who know you professionally and can speak about your performance and work ethic. Last but not least for employer-related references, you can consider your peers. However, peers should be limited to one out of your three total professional references.

Once you have exhausted employer-oriented references, you can look at educators and university professors, as well as community leaders you have met through your networking and affiliations. For instance, if you sit on a board of directors, volunteer for an organization, or belong to a local chapter of your professional association, you might have developed some high-level industry contacts that would be able to act as your references.

Finally, you can consider professional friends of the family followed by longtime personal friends as your last option. As with your peers, however, personal and family friends should be limited to only one of your three professional references.

When selecting your references, do not pick people just because of their standing in the community or the name recognition they can offer. Although those are definite pluses, they are not enough if the individual is not able to talk about your strengths, skills, and value to an employer.

All in all, pick your three professional references carefully, educate them on your job search, and stay in regular communication to keep them abreast of any changes in your experience or targets. That way, the next time you are asked for references, you will be ready to make a positive impression on the prospective employer.

Choose Your References Carefully

Job Seeker's Story

Carolyn graduated from college in May with a 3.75 GPA in Liberal Arts with a major in Social Sciences. She had prepared her résumé and cover letter according to the guidelines the college's career counseling office gave her, and consulted her dad about the references she should have. Because he felt that professional community members have a lot of influence, Carolyn's dad suggested she list the minister of the church they attended, the local realtor, and the vice president of the bank—all of whom Carolyn's dad knew well.

Carolyn spent the summer conducting her job search, going on interviews, working part-time at the weight-loss clinic in the local hospital, and volunteering with the community center. None of her interviews led to any job offers, and Carolyn started to get worried in September that her job search would be a never-ending process.

One day, at the weight-loss clinic, Carolyn met Clair, the Realtor she had been using as a reference, who remarked that she had gotten several reference-check calls from potential employers inquiring about Carolyn. She said she had praised Carolyn as a "nice girl" from a good family, but really could not say more about Carolyn's career goals or particular abilities, although each employer had pressed her for such information.

Job Seeker's Stumble

Although professional community members can potentially be excellent references, your references need to be people who know you and can comment on your goals, accomplishments, and singular attributes based on their experience with you.

Job Seeker's ≥New Strategy≤

Carolyn would have done better considering references from the three tiers of people she knew well and who could comment on her potential value to an employer:

▷ **Tier 1: People 1 or More Levels Above You:** Because she had been working on a regular basis for four months at the weight-loss clinic, Carolyn's supervisor had gotten to know Carolyn well and was impressed with her maturity, good decision-making ability, organizational skills, and enthusiastic attitude. At the local community center, the Center Director thought Carolyn was one of the best volunteers they had ever had—a real team player, highly computer literate, and a pleasure to be around. Carolyn's professors remembered her as studious and smart, and eager to help others who were struggling in the course by giving them individual tutoring and establishing a study group.

▷ **Tier 2: People at the Same Level as You:** Carolyn's co-workers at the weight-loss clinic had come to rely on Carolyn for her creative problem-solving and her willingness to always help out. Other volunteers at the community center were similarly struck by Carolyn's helpfulness, leadership qualities, and enthusiastic *joie de vivre*. Some of these volunteers were influential community members.

▷ **Tier 3: People 1 Level Below You:** Carolyn did not supervise anyone; however, she did serve diverse populations in the weight-loss clinic and the community center. Although only in the job a few months, Carolyn had already received many cards and letters of thanks from people she had cared about and helped. One such person was someone who had tried twice before to lose weight unsuccessfully, but whom Carolyn had coached in losing 30 pounds in five months.

By choosing two or three people from Tier 1 and one to two each in Tier 2 and Tier 3, Carolyn could have accessed more appropriate references with substantial and heartfelt recommendations. This 360-degree approach to selecting references allows the prospective employer to obtain feedback about you from varied perspectives, all of which could serve to reinforce your brand differentiation and corroborate your skills and market value.

List of Contributors

⌄

All of the contributors to this book, including the co-authors, are career professionals who belong to the industry's leading professional association, Career Directors International. Their career specialties range from résumé writing and career coaching to human resources. We have provided their contact information here. A legend of certification acronyms follows.

Co-Authors

Laura DeCarlo
Career Directors International, Executive Director
A Competitive Edge Career Service, LLC
    1665 Clover Circle
    Melbourne, FL 32935
    Phone: (321) 752–0880
    E-mail:
    success@acompetitiveedge.com
    Website:
    www.acompetitiveedge.com
    Credentials: BS, MCD, CERW, CECC, CCMC, CCM, CEIC, IJCTC, CCRE, CWPP, 360Reach

Susan Guarneri
Guarneri Associates
    6670 Crystal Lake Road
    Three Lakes, WI 54562
    Phone: (715) 546–4449
    E-mail:
    susan@assessmentgoddess.com
    Website:
    www.assessmentgoddess.com
    Credentials: MS, NCC, NCCC, LPC, MCC, DCC, CCMC, CPBS, COIMS, CERW, CPRW, CEIP, IJCTC, 360Reach

Additional Contributors

The following professionals contributed many of the blooper stories included in this book. We acknowledge with gratitude their voluntary submissions and support.

Arnold G. Boldt
Arnold-Smith Associates
   625 Panorama Trail
   Building One, Suite 120
   Rochester, NY 14625
   Phone: (585) 383–0350
   E-mail: Arnie@ResumeSOS.com
   Website: *www.ResumeSOS.com*
   Credentials: CPRW, CJCTC

Nita Busby
Resumes, Etc.
   438 E. Katella, Suite G
   Orange, CA 92867
   Phone: (714) 633–2783
   E-mail: Resumes100@aol.com
   Website: *www.resumesetc.net*
   Credentials: CAC, BA, MSLS, CJCTC

Camille Carboneau Roberts
CC Computer Services & Training
   P.O. Box 50655
   Idaho Falls, ID 83405
   Phone: (208) 522–4455
   E-mail: Camille@SuperiorResumes.com
   Website: *www.SuperiorResumes.com*
   Credentials: CFRWC, CPRW, CEIP, CARW, CCRE

Freddie Cheek
Cheek & Associates
   406 Maynard Drive
   Amherst, NY 14226
   Phone: (716) 835–6945
   E-mail: fscheek@cheekandassociates.com
   Website: *www.cheekandassociates.com*
   Credentials: MS.Ed., CCM, CPRW, CARW, CWDP

Tony Deblauwe
HR4Change
   Millbrae, CA 94030
   Phone: (650) 455–6806
   E-mail: hr4change@yahoo.com
   Website: *www.hr4change.com*
   Credentials: MHROD, CCRE, MCD, CLC, CEC

Tamara Dowling
SeekingSuccess.com
   23890 Copper Hill Drive, #199
   Valencia, CA 91354
   Phone: (661) 903–0696
   E-mail: td@SeekingSuccess.com
   Website: *www.SeekingSuccess.com*
   Credentials: CPRW

Michelle La Faunge-Berns
Strategic Talent Coach
   12674-44 Carmel Country Road
   San Diego, CA 92130
   Phone: (858) 254–2083
   E-mail: StrategicTalentCoach@gmail.com
   Website: *www.michelleberns.com*
   Credentials: CSC, PNLPP

Marilyn A. Feldstein
Career Choices Unlimited
   4465 Baymeadows Road, Suite 7
   Jacksonville, FL 32217
   Phone: (904) 443–0059/(904) 262–9470
   E-mail: mfeldstein@bellsouth.net
   Website: *www.careerchoicesunlimited.com*
   Credentials: MPA, CJCTC, MBTI, PHR

Susan Geary
1st Rate Resumes
   1443 Lynchburg Turnpike
   Salem, VA 24153
   Phone: (866) 690–4622
   E-mail: info@1stRateResumes.com
   Website: *www.1stRateResumes.com*
   Credentials: CERW, CEIC, CARW, CPRW

Meg Guiseppi
Résumés Plus LLC
   13 Perona Road
   Andover, NJ 07821
   Phone: (973) 726–0757
   E-mail: megguiseppi@resumesplusllc.com
   Website: *www.ExecutiveResumeBranding.com*
   Credentials: CPRW, MRW

Cindy Hastings
employment CHOICE
   P.O. Box 71
   Bonny Hills, New South Wales, Australia
   Phone: 61 2 6585 5941
   E-mail: cindy@employmentchoice.com.au
   Website: *www.employmentchoice.com.au*
   Credentials: CARW

Gayle M. Howard
Top Margin
   P.O. Box 74
   Chirnside Park 3116
   Melbourne, Australia
   Phone: 61 3 9726 6694
   E-mail: getinterviews@topmargin.com
   Website: *www.topmargin.com*
   Credentials: MCD, CERW, CCM, CMRS, CARW, CPRW,
   CWPP

Jill Kelly
Career Edge
   147 Redland Bay Road
   Capalaba, Queensland, Australia
   Phone: 61 7 3824 5200
   E-mail: jill@careeredge.com.au
   Website: *www.careeredge.com.au*
   Credentials: B.Bus, P.Grad Adult Vocational Education,
   CARW, CERW

Laura Labovich
A & E Consulting, LLC
   Potomac Falls, VA

Phone: (703) 942–9390
E-mail: aspireempower@gmail.com
Website: *www.aspire-empower.com*
Certifications: CARW, CFRW, CCM

Malloy Lacktman
Sage Resumes
  9963 Santa Monica Boulevard
  Beverly Hills, CA 90210
  Phone: (888) 625–5695
  E-mail: Malloy@SageResumes.com
  Website: *www.SageResumes.com*
  Credentials: BBA

Eva Locke
Lake County Workforce Development
  1 N. Genesee Street
  Waukegan, IL 60085
  Phone: (847) 377–3456
  E-mail: elocke@co.lake.il.us
  Website: *www.lakecountyjobcenter.com*
  Credentials: CARW

Jay Markunas
Great Occupation
  P.O. Box 20155
  Austin, TX 78720
  Phone: (877) 473–2813
  E-mail: jay@greatoccupation.com
  Website: *www.greatoccupation.com*

Nona Pratz
Types Write
  433 Metairie Road, Suite 117
  Metairie, LA 70005
  Phone: (504) 835–5039
  E-mail: typeswrite@aol.com
  Credentials: CARW, CPRW, CCRE

Jane Roqueplot
JaneCo's Sensible Solutions
  194 North Oakland Avenue
  Sharon, PA 16146

Phone: (724) 342–0100
E-mail: jane@janecos.com
Website: *www.janecos.com*
Credentials: CPBA, CWDP, CECC

Barbara Safani
Career Solvers
470 Park Avenue South, 10th Floor
New York, NY 10016
Phone: (866) 333–1800
E-mail: info@careersolvers.com
Website: *www.careersolvers.com*
Certifications: MA, CERW, NCRW, CPRW, CCM

Robin Schlinger
Robin's Resumes
860 Peachtree Street NE, #2206
Atlanta, GA 30308
Phone: (404) 875–2688
E-mail: robinschlinger@robinresumes.com
Website: *www.robinresumes.com*
Credentials: CARW, CFRW, CECC

Kimberly Schneiderman
City Career Services
New York, NY 10022
Phone: (917) 584–3022
E-mail: kimberly@citycareerservices.com
Website: *www.citycareerservices.com*
Credentials: CEIC, NCRW

Laura Smith-Proulx
An Expert Resume
15400 West 64th Avenue, Suite E9 #164
Arvada, CO 80007
Phone: (877) 258–3517
E-mail: laura@anexpertresume.com
Website: *www.anexpertresume.com*
Credentials: CPRW, CIC

Bob Simmons
Career Transition Associates (CTA)
  1670 Old Country Road, Suite 117
  Plainview, NY 11803
  Phone: (516) 501–0717
  E-mail: Ctasimmons@aol.com
  Website: *www.ctajobsearch.com*
  Credentials: BBA

Donald B. Skipper
Career Beginnings, Inc.
  P.O. Box 870941
  Stone Mountain, GA 30087
  Phone: (770) 922–6161
  E-mail: dskipper@nofeartransitions.us
  Website: *www.nofeartransitions.us*
  Credentials: CCM, MCD, CEIC, CECC, CCTC

Marilyn Stollon
  400 29th Street, Suite 102
  Oakland, CA 94609
  Phone: (510) 987–7271
  E-mail: ms@findworkNow.org
  Website: *www.findworkNow.org*
  Credentials: BA

Joellyn Wittenstein Schwerdlin
Career-Success-Coach.com
  40 Chippewa Road
  Worcester, MA 01602
  Phone: (508) 459–2854
  E-mail: joellyn@career-success-coach.com
  Website: *www.career-success-coach.com/*
  Credentials: CCMC, CJCTC, CPRW

Faith Evan West
Higher Ground Coaching
  Dundas, Ontario, Canada
  E-mail: highergroundcoaching@cogeco.ca
  Website: *www.uniqueology.com*
  Credentials: ATC

Credentials Legend

Credentials bestowed by Career Directors International are indicated with an asterisk (*).

360Reach—360Reach Personal Branding Assessment

ATC—Adler Trained Coach

BA—Bachelor of Arts

BBA—Bachelor of Business Administration

B.Bus—Bachelor of Business Management

BS—Bachelor of Science Degree

CAC—California Accredited Consultant

CARW—Certified Advanced Résumé Writer*

CCM—Credentialed Career Manager

CCMC—Certified Career Management Coach

CCRE—Certified Career Research Expert*

CCTC—Corrections Career Transition Certified*

CEC—Certified Executive Coach

CECC—Certified Electronic Career Coach*

CEIC—Certified Employment Interview Consultant*

CEIP—Certified Employment Interview Professional

CERW—Certified Expert Résumé Writer*

CFRW—Certified Federal Résumé Writer*

CFRWC—Certified Federal Résumé Writer/Coach

CIC—Certified Interview Consultant

CJCTC—Certified Job & Career Transition Coach

CLC—Certified Life Coach

COIMS—Certified Online Identity Management Strategist

CPBA—Certified Professional Behavioral Analyst

CPBS—Certified Personal Branding Strategist

CMRS—Certified Master Resume Specialist

CPRW—Certified Professional Résumé Writer

CSC—Certified Success Coach

CWDP—Certified Workforce Development Professional

CWPP—Certified Web Portfolio Practitioner*

DCC—Distance Career Counselor

IJCTC—International Job & Career Transition Coach

LPC—Licensed Professional Counselor

MA—Master of Arts

MBTI—Myers-Briggs Type Indicator

MCC—Master Career Counselor

MCD—Master Career Director*

MHROD—Masters in Human Resources and Organizational Development

MPA—Master of Public Administration

MRW—Master Résumé Writer

MS—Master of Science Degree

MS.Ed.—Master of Science in Education

MSLS—Master of Science in Library Science

NCC—National Certified Counselor

NCCC—National Certified Career Counselor

NCRW—Nationally Certified Résumé Writer

P.Grad Adult Vocational Education—Post Graduate Diploma in Adult & Vocational Education

PHR—Professional in Human Resources

PNLPP—Professional Neuro Linguistic Programming (NLP) Practitioner

Career Directors International

Career Directors International (CDI) is the career professionals' professional association, dedicated to providing the education, training, research, and global networking needed to help job seekers succeed. CDI is the founder of international registered events including *Update Your Résumé Month* and *Update Your References Week.* The association offers 10 certifications in specialties ranging from résumé writing and Web portfolio development to career coaching and career research. CDI pioneered the highly recognized industry report series *Career Industry Mega Trends,* a major resource of breaking new trends for career professionals and job seekers.

CDI's global membership spans all career disciplines and includes résumé writers, career coaches and counselors, job developers, recruiters, outplacement specialists, human resources practitioners, and other specialists from private practice, civil service, academia, and military.

Contact Career Directors International for more information:

Career Directors International
1665 Clover Circle
Melbourne, FL 32935
Phone: (321) 752–0442/Toll-Free (888) 867–7972
E-mail: info@careerdirectors.com
Website: *www.careerdirectors.com*

Cited Online Resources

∧

360Reach Personal Branding assessment	*www.reachcc.com/360register*
About.com	*www.about.com*
Accountemps	*www.accountemps.com*
Advanced Google Search	*www.google.com/ advanced_search*
AIRS Directory	*www.airsdirectory.com*
Alta Vista	*www.altavista.com*
American Society for Quality	*www.asq.org*
American Society of Mechanical Engineers (ASME)	*www.asme.org*
America's Career InfoNet	*www.acinet.org/acinet/*
America's Career InfoNet Employer Finder	*www.acinet.org/acinet/ employerlocator/ employerlocator.asp*
AssessmentGoddess.com	*www.assessmentgoddess.com*
AssociationJobBoards.com	*www.associationjobboards.com*
Avoiding Online Job Scams	*www.privacyrights.org/fs/fs25a-jobSeekerPriv2.htm*
Best Careers 2008 (*U.S. News & World Report*)	*www.usnews.com/features/ business/best-careers/best-careers-2008.html*
Better Business Bureau	*www.bbbonline.org*
BigCharts	*www.bigcharts.com*

The Brand Called You	*www.fastcompany.com/magazine/10/brandyou.html*
Brand You World! Personal Branding Summit	*w.personalbrandingsummit.com*
Bureau of Labor Statistics	*www.bls.gov*
Business.com	*www.business.com*
Business Journal	*www.bizjournals.com*
Business Wire	*www.businesswire.com*
CareerBuilder	*www.careerbuilder.com*
Career Directors International (CDI)	*www.careerdirectors.com*
Career Focus Quiz	*www.assessmentgoddess.com/careerfocusquiz.html*
Career Goddess Blog	*blog.careergoddess.com/*
Career Guide to Industries	*www.bls.gov/oco/cg/*
CareerHub	*careerhub.typepad.com*
Career Journal	*www.careerjournal.com*
CareerOneStop	*careeronestop.org*
CareerOneStop—Explore Careers	*www.careeronestop.org/ExploreCareers/ExploreCareers.aspx*
Career Voyages	*www.careervoyages.gov/*
CareerXRoads	*www.careerxroads.com*
CEOExpress	*www.ceoexpress.com*
Clusty	*clusty.com*
CNN Money	*money.cnn.com*
College Search on CollegeNET	*cnsearch.collegenet.com/cgi-bin/CN/index*
Corporate Alumni	*www.corporatealumni.com*
Corporate Directory of U.S. Public Companies (fee)	*www.researchandmarkets.com/reports/302094*
	www.amazon.com/Corporate-Directory-Us-Public-Companies/dp/B00006KA9P

Corporate Information	*www.corporateinformation.com*
Craigslist	*www.craigslist.com*
Crosswalk Search	*online.onetcenter.org/crosswalk/*
DisabilityInfo	*www.disabilityinfo.gov/digov-public/public/DisplayPage.do?parentFolderId=500*
Ecademy	*www.ecademy.com*
Edgar Online	*www.edgar-online.com*
Employability Check-up	*www.acinet.org/acinet/employabilitycheckup/emp_ask.asp*
EmploymentGuide.com	*www.employmentguide.com*
Encyclopedia of Associations	*library.dialog.com/bluesheets/html/bl0114.html*
Engineer.net	*www.engineer.net*
ExecuNet	*www.execunet.com*
Experience	*www.experience.com*
Facebook	*www.facebook.com*
Fast Company	*www.fastcompany.com*
Federal Citizen's Information Center (FCIC) for Scams and Frauds	*www.pueblo.gsa.gov/scamsdesc.htm*
Federal Jobs by Major	*www.usajobs.opm.gov/ei23.asp*
Fortune 500	*money.cnn.com/magazines/fortune/fortune500/*
Fortune Magazine	*www.fortune.com*
Gateway to Associations	*www.asaecenter.org/Directories/AssociationSearch.cfm?navItemNumber=16581*
Global 500	*money.cnn.com/magazines/fortune/global500/2006/*
Google Blog Search	*blogsearch.google.com*
Google Finance	*finance.google.com*
Hoovers	*www.hoovers.com*
Idealist Guide to Non-Profit Careers	*www.idealist.org/careerguide*

Inc. 500	*www.inc.com/inc5000/index.html*
Indeed	*www.indeed.com*
Internet Public Library	*www.ipl.org*
Jaycees	*www.usjaycees.org*
JibberJobber	*www.jibberjobber.com*
Job-Hunt	*www.job-hunt.org*
JobsInManufacturing.com	*www.jobsinmanufacturing.com*
JobStar Salary Guide	*www.jobstar.org/tools/salary/sal-prof.php*
Kennedy Guide to Executive Recruiters (fee)	*www.recruiterredbook.com/index.php*
LinkedIn	*www.linkedin.com*
Lion's Clubs	*www.lionsclubs.org*
List of Lists	*www.specialissues.com/lol*
Local Careers	*www.localcareers.com*
Local Employment Dynamics	*lehd.did.census.gov/led/datatools/datatools.html*
MagPortal	*www.magportal.com*
MarketWatch	*www.marketwatch.com*
Match a Major to Job Listings	*6steps.monster.com/step1/careerconverter*
MechanicalEngineer.com	*www.mechanicalengineer.com*
Mechanical Engineering Magazine	*www.memagazine.org*
Medical Devicelink	*www.devicelink.com*
Michigan Newspapers	*www.newslink.org/minews.html*
Michigan Talent Bank	*www.michworks.org*
Monster	*www.monster.com*
MSN Money	*moneycentral.msn.com*
MyReferences.com	*www.myreferences.com*
MySpace	*www.myspace.com*
National Society for Professional Engineers	*www.nspe.org*

NASDAQ Trader	*www.nasdaqtrader.com*
News Directory	*www.newsdirectory.com*
News Link	*www.newslink.org/mbiz.html*
NicheBoards.com	*www.nicheboards.com*
Occupational Outlook Handbook	*www.bls.gov/oco/home.htm*
Occupational Outlook Quarterly	*www.bls.gov/opub/ooq/ooqindex.html*
OfficeTeam	*www.officeteam.com*
O'NET Center	*www.onetcenter.org*
O'NET Career Exploration Tools	*www.onetcenter.org/tools.html*
O'NET Online	*online.onetcenter.org*
Online Identity Calculator	*www.careerdistinction.com/onlineid*
Pacific Information Resources, Inc.	*www.pac-info.com*
Payscale	*www.payscale.com*
Personal Branding Blog	*ww.thepersonalbrandingblog.com*
Personal Branding Quiz	*www.assessmentgoddess.com/brandingquiz.html*
Plaxo	*www.plaxo.com*
Private 500	*www.forbes.com/fdc/welcome_mjx.shtml*
Quintessential Careers	*www.quintessentialcareers.com*
Reach Branding Club	*www.reachbrandingclub.com*
Reach Communications	*www.reachcc.com*
Recruiters Online Network	*recruitersonline.com*
Regional Economic Conditions (RECON)	*www2.fdic.gov/recon*
Resume-Magic.com	*www.resume-magic.com*
Reuters	*vwww.reuters.com*
Richard Bolles's *What Color Is Your Parachute?*	*www.jobhuntersbible.com*
Rotary Club	*www.rotary.org*
Ryze	*www.ryze.com*

Salary.com	*www.salary.com*
Salary Expert	*www.salaryexpert.com*
Salary Scout	*www.salaryscout.com*
SEC Info	*www.secinfo.com*
Simply Hired	*www.simplyhired.com*
Skills Profiler	*www.careerinfonet.org/skills*
Society of Automotive Engineers	*www.sae.org*
Society of Human Resource Managers	*www.shrm.org*
Technorati	*www.technorati.com*
ThomasNet	*www.thomasnet.com/index.html*
Toastmasters International	*www.toastmasters.org*
Topix	*www.topix.com*
Tribe	*www.tribe.com*
USAJobs	*www.usajobs.gov*
U.S. Attorney General's Office	*www.usdoj.gov/ag*
U.S. Chamber of Commerce	*uschamber.com*
Vault	*www.vault.com*
Vocation Vacations	*www.vocationvacation.com*
Wetfeet.com	*www.wetfeet.com*
Yahoo! Finance	*finance.yahoo.com*
Yahoo Finance Global Ticker Symbol Lookup	*quote.yahoo.com/lookup*
Yahoo! HotJobs	*www.hotjobs.com*
Zoominfo	*www.zoominfo.com*

References

"Albert Mehrabian: Three Elements of Communication—and the '7%-38%-55% Rule.'" Wikipedia.com. *en.wikipedia.org/wiki/ Albert_Mehrabian*. Accessed January 2008.

Bureau of Labor Statistics. *The Career Guide to Industries, Sources of State and Local Job Outlook Information. www.bls.gov/oco/cg/ cgjobout.htm*. Accessed February 2008.

———. "Employee Tenure Summary." Online news release, September 8, 2006. *www.bls.gov/news/release/tenure.nr0.htm*. Accessed February 2008.

———.*Quarterly Census of Employment & Wages (QCEW). www.bls.gov/cew/home.htm*. Accessed February 2008.

Bureau of Labor Statistics, National Longitudinal Surveys. "NLS Frequently Asked Questions." Online posting. *www.bls.gov/ NLS/nlsfaqs.htm#anch41*. Accessed February 2008.

Bureau of Labor Statistics, North American Industry Classification System (NAICS). "NAICS Coding Structure." Online posting, December 21, 2007. *www.bls.gov/bls/naics.htm*. Accessed January 2008.

Crispin, Gerry, and Mark Mehler. "CareerXRoads Research: 7th Annual Source of Hire Study." 2007 CareerXRoads online article. *www.careerxroads.com/news/SOHResults.asp*. Accessed February 2008.

"Don't Forget the Spell-Check: Survey Finds a Single Résumé Typo Can Ruin Job Prospects." OfficeTeam online press release, September 6, 2006. *tinyurl.com/32zxtk*. Accessed September 2007.

Enelow, Wendy. "Statistical Data on Social Networks." The Career Management Alliance E-Bridge online newsletter (members only), Issue #395, December 3, 2007. *www.careermanagementalliance.com.* Accessed December 2007.

Franco, Lynn. "U.S. Job Satisfaction Declines, The Conference Board Reports." The Conference Board online press release, February 23, 2007. *www.conference-board.org/utilities/pressDetail.cfm?press_ID=3075.* Accessed March 2007.

Frauenheim, Ed. "Studies: More Workers Look to Switch Jobs." Workforce.com, February 22, 2006. *www.workforce.com/section/00/article/24/28/08.html.* Accessed February 2008.

Gioia-Herman, Joyce. "2007 Workforce/Workplace Forecast—The Herman Group." *Recruiting News*, Vol. 9, Issue 1, January 24, 2007. *www.recruitersnetwork.com/news/issue.cfm?Newsletter=1.* Accessed January 2008.

Greenspan, Robyn. "ExecuNet Career Guide: Dealing with Your Digital Dirt v2.5." ExecutNet online white paper (members only), 2007. *www.execunet.com.* Accessed September 2007.

Hadley, Kathy, and Judy Ware. "Background Investigations and Privacy, Career Industry Mega Trends: What You and Your Clients Need to Know." Career Director's International 2006–2007 Research Study. Melbourne, Fla.: Career Director's International, 2007.

"Multiple Careers." Wikipedia.com, February 2008. *en.wikipedia.org/wiki/Multiple_Careers.* Accessed February 2008.

"SHRM 2006 Access to Human Capital and Employment Verification Survey Report." Society for Human Resource Management (SHRM) online survey report (members only), March 1, 2006. *www.shrm.org/hrresources/surveys_published/bydate/.* Accessed March 2006.

"SHRM Cover Letters & Resume Survey." Society for Human Resource Management online survey report (members only), May 2000. *www.shrm.org/hrresources/surveys_published/archive/.* Accessed January 2008.

"Thanks, But No Thanks." Accountemps online press release, August 9, 2007. *tinyurl.com/6m9sy2.* Accessed February 2008.

Index

accomplishments, 66, 118, 136
Accountemps, 99
achievement-focused bullets, 38
adult internship, 164
Applicant Tracking Systems (ATS), 113
application,
    confirming receipt of your, 19
    job, 18
application addendum, 15
appropriate gestures, 199
appropriateness, 91
arriving too early, 203
asking questions, 186-187
auto-responder programs, 20-21
background checks, 34
bad-mouthing a former employer, 182, 184
bite-sized content, 45-46
body language, 196-198
bolding, 59
boring job description, 36
bragging, 194-195
brand differentiation, 232
bribe, attempting a, 93
business cards, 96
buzzwords, 55
capitalization, 59
C-A-R- format, 161
career
    assessment, formal, 163
    coach, 161, 165, 167, 186, 196, 215
    counselor, 165
    focus, 135
Career Directors International, 9
career-advancing courses, 70
career-discovery tools, 160
career-target consistency, 114
CareerXRoads, 113, 207
casual organizations, 214
C-C-A-R
    formula, 41-43
    stories, 195, 208
certifications, 27
chronology of work history, detailed, 14
classified ads, 109
combination format, 65
community involvement, 28
company
    and industry research, 167
    culture, 42, 195
    history, 189
compensation questions, 17
computer skills, 28
confirming receipt of your application, 19
contact information,76
cost of living, 224
courtesy, showing, 129
cover letter,
    generic, 82
    targeted, 82
cover letters, 73-88
creativity, 89-91

credibility, 135-137
culture fit, 209
dating your experience, 66
depression, 125
direction, providing clear, 47
directions, an unwillingness to follow, 17
distinctiveness, 135-137
documentation, bring sufficient, 15
dress
    for success, 15
    to fit in, 212-214
due diligence, 108-109
Early Experience section, 68
Education section, 59
education, 25, 27
ego, separating, 51
elevator pitch, the, 151-152
emotional intelligence, lack of, 156
employee referrals, 113, 125
employment gaps, 35
employment-reviewer confusion, 114
entitlement attitude, 17
entry-level job, 22
equal employment opportunities, 18
etiquette, networking, 158
experience, dating your, 66
"eye time," 64
fabricating career information, 34
Facebook, 152, 169, 192
falsified
    credentials, 35
    employment status, 33
family-owned business, 40
feedback, elicit specific, 21
financials, check, 189
first impressions, 13-15, 85, 179-181
five-step career planning process, 163
flight risk, 48
following
    instructions, 18
    up, 19
follow-up,
    schedule a, 20
    timely, 142
follow-up letters, 89-100
food, bringing to an interview, 180

fraud, 108
functional
    categories, using, 45
    format, 63, 65
    strategy, 45-46
gaps, five types of, 69
gaps in the timeline, 68
generic résumés, 137
geographic regions, 224
good
    cop, bad cop, 210
    manners, 194
grammatical errors, 32, 77
handwriting analysis, 97
health limitation, 185
hiding career information, 34
hiring bonuses, 113
hobbies and awards, 29
    inappropriate, 72
honesty, 184-185
humor, attempt at, 23
I, the word, 74
illness, not working due to an, 70
informational
    interview, 144-155, 216
    interviewing, 164
    interviews, 146, 160-161
interim jobs, 13
internal transfers, 207
Internet job postings, 159
interview
    coaching, 196
    outfit, 201
    preparation, 200-202
interviewing wardrobe, 132
introductory paragraph, 39
JibberJobber, 145, 153
job
    clubs, 126
    description, 41
    description, boring, 36
    descriptions, 37-38
    fair, 119-122, 125, 213
    history, 28
    hopper, 64
    hopping, 167
    leads, 143, 150

search action plan, 126
search group, 126
search isolation, 126
search plan, 131
shadowing, 164
targets, 226
targets, different, 134
targets, résumés with different, 114
key takeaways, 43
Keyword section, 49, 52
keywords, 27, 55, 62, 161
leadership, 28
leaving dates off, 67
legal issues, 15
life/balance concerns, 165
life-balance needs, 126
likability factor, 209
LinkedIn, 144, 152-153, 169, 192
lying on résumés, 34
making demands, 217
mannerisms, 197
    negative, 197-198
market value, your, 232
misinterpretation, 97
misspellings, 31
mistakes in descriptions, two key, 37
mixed message, 197
multiple résumés, 113-114
MySpace, 152
name-calling, 184
negative
    comments, 181
    impression, 127
negatives, addressing, 80
network, your, 192
networking, 105, 110, 126, 143-158, 160,
    164, 224, 230
    appropriate situations for, 156
    online and offline, 125
networking
    buddy, 151
    contacts, professional, 109
    meetings, 227
non-negotiable requirements, 117
nonverbal behavior, 197
Objective statement, the, 48-50, 53, 110, 136
OCR scanners, 59

OfficeTeam, 31
online
    career-management system, 145
    resources, 164
    social networking, 192
optional sections, 59
out-of-the-box approaches, 90
over-pricing yourself, 24
over-qualified, being, 72
passive
    responsibilities, 37
    responsibility content, 36
personal
    brand, your, 54, 56, 163, 165
    branding, 43, 136-137, 160,
        175-178, 209
    branding assessment, online, 55
    business cards, 132
    credibility, 114
    style, understand your, 133
personal-branding portfolio, 161
personalization, 93
positive impression, leave a, 14
post-interview phase, the, 100
pre-qualifying your suitability, 119
professional
    interview behavior, 192-196
    networking contacts, 109
    references, 225-23
    résumé writer, 173
professionalism, 14, 181, 183-184, 194,
    196, 199, 211-212
proof of value, 172-173
proofread, 78
    your résumé, 32
proofreading, 79
rapport, 208
Reach Branding Club, the, 55
reasons for leaving, 29
recruiters, 102, 125
Reference Data Sheet, 30
references, 29
referrals, ask for, 155
reimbursement arrangements, 201
résumé,
    extra copies of, 16
    proofread your, 32

résumé
    overkill, 28
    reviewers, 44
    writing professional, 18
résumés with different job targets, 114
reverse chronological format, 65
reviewer's time, showing consideration for the, 76
right-sizing program, 106
role-playing, 161, 215
Ryze, 169
sabbatical, a, 70
salary, low, 221
salary
    bracket, higher, 220
    compensation sites, 216
    expectations, 215
    history, 29, 86-87
    negotiation, 218
    negotiations, 24, 224
    offer, the first, 219
    ranges, 102
    research, 23-24
    survey guides, 224
scam operation, 108
scannable presentation, 58
script, have a, 137-138
selective marketing document, résumé as a, 27, 30
self-centered, being, 74
self-confidence, 131, 160
    excessive, 99
self-employment, 164
self-esteem, 130
selfish focus, 48
self-knowledge, 16
self-marketing, 99
self-marketing content, 74
self-serving content, 48
self-worth, loss of, 125
social
    intelligence, 157
    interactions, 150
    networking sites, 106
    networking Websites, 169
staffing agencies, 125

strengths, lead with your, 64
Summary section, 30-31, 45, 49, 53-56, 65, 176
support
    network, 126
    system, 129-133
    team, 132-133
Tagline, 176
talent development and retention, 207
target marketing, 16, 72
targeted
    job search campaign, 119
    responses, 83
team
    culture, 42
    dynamics, 178
team-player attitude, 18
techno-speak, 50
template e-mails, 145
temporary agencies, 10
thank-you letters, 95, 211
360Reach Assessment, 55
360Reach Personal Branding Assessment, 178
titled bullet strategy, 46
Toastmasters, 151
Toastmasters International, 146
top-loading your résumé, 55
total compensation benchmark, 223
training, 27
typos, 31-32, 77-78
ultimatum, 218
undervaluing yourself, 24
unemployment, 70
Unique Selling Proposition (USP), 54
unprofessional attitude, 127
valuable accomplishments, 174
value proposition, 54
visual
    presentation, 58
    strategies, overuse of, 59
volunteering, 70, 164
warm leads, 40, 144, 153
weaknesses, 203-206
W-I-I-F-M résumé, 39-43

About the Authors

SUSAN GUARNERI, the "Career Assessment Goddess," has a master's degree in counseling from The Johns Hopkins University, plus 23 years of experience in career counseling and coaching. She has assisted Fortune 500 companies, colleges, and government agencies with management development, team building, career-development consulting, training, and workforce development.

Susan is the only National Certified Career Counselor worldwide also certified as a Personal Branding Strategist and Online Identity Management Strategist. She writes the Career Goddess Blog (blog.careergoddess .com/), and is a guest blogger for Personal Branding Blog and CareerHub blog. In addition, she is a certified Distance Career Counselor and Master Resume Writer with a Lifetime Achievement Award from Career Directors International. She holds 13 certifications in career counseling, online coaching, career management, personal branding, online identity management, international job search and career transition, interview coaching, and résumé writing.

She is the author of the New Jersey SUCCESS Program for women re-entering the workforce, as well as the New York City Summer Youth Employment Training Program. Susan has been featured in diverse media, such as Monster.com, Careerbuilder.com, Careerjournal.com, the *Princeton Business Journal*, the *Atlanta Journal Constitution*, *New Jersey News*, Richard Bolles's (author of *What Color Is Your Parachute?*) Radio Show, and the *Career Planning and Adult Development Journal*, as well as more than 40 professional association publications and best-selling books.

Susan's leadership roles include being one of the principle organizers for the Brand You World! Personal Branding Summit in November 2007, 360Reach Leadership Team, Reach Branding Club Teleseminar Series Producer, and a number of board of director positions. Her Websites include AssessmentGoddess.com and Resume-Magic.com.

Laura DeCarlo offers 16 years of expertise in résumé writing, career coaching, and career management as Executive Director of A Competitive Edge Career Service, LLC, a turnkey career services firm, and President of Career Directors International, an innovative association of career professionals.

She has attained 10 industry certifications, including Master Career Director, Certified Expert Résumé Writer, Credentialed Career Manager, Certified Job & Career Transition Coach, Certified Electronic Career Coach, Certified Web Portfolio Practitioner, Certified Career Management Coach, Certified Career Research Expert, and Certified Employment Interview Consultant, and 360Reach Personal Branding Assessment administrator. She also possesses a BA in creative/technical writing, and extensive graduate studies in human resources, training, and counseling.

Laura is a résumé writing expert for 54 professional associations worldwide, such as PMI, AMA, AJST, ASAE, ASME, and ASCE. She is the author of *Interviewing: The Gold Standard* program and the book *Interview Pocket RX*, and has been published in 15-plus résumé/cover letter compendiums. She has won seven awards, including the Master Résumé Writer Lifetime Achievement Award. She has also pioneered industry education, outreach, and recognition programs such as the Certified Employment Interview Consultant course, Certified Web Portfolio Practitioner course, and annual Career Industry Mega Trends research reports.

Other accomplishments include nationwide transition programs for organizations such as the U.S. Treasury, national conference speaking engagements, former guest columnist for the *Florida Today* newspaper, and Director of Placement for Herzing College. She has been quoted in publications such as *Forbes (IMPRESS)*, *Working Mother*, and the *Wall Street Journal*, and appeared on NBC 7/39 News in San Diego and Wall Street Journal Radio.